THE WORLD OF
OZ

THE WORLD OF
OZ

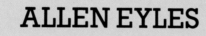

ALLEN EYLES

HPBooks

First published in the United States in 1985 by HPBooks Inc., P.O. Box 5367, Tucson, AZ 85703 (602/888-2150)

ISBN: 0-89586-415-0
Library of Congress Catalog Card Number: 85-60487

Created, designed and produced by Black Pig Editions Ltd.
(Justin Knowles Publishing Group), P.O. Box 99, Exeter, Devon, England.

Cover design by HPBooks

For Black Pig Editions:
Editor: Mike Darton   Design: Roger Huggett
Production: Nick Facer

For HPBooks:
Publisher: Rick Bailey   Editorial Director: Randy Summerlin   Editor: Judith Schuler

Typeset by P&M Typesetting Ltd, Exeter, England.
Printed and bound in Hong Kong by Mandarin Offset Ltd.

Notice: The information in this book is true and complete to the best of our knowledge.
All recommendations are made without guarantee on the part of the
author or HPBooks. The author and publisher disclaim all liability
in connection with the use of the information.

First American edition.

Publisher's Acknowledgments

The catalytic Keith Bales of Walt Disney Productions initiated our interest in the "World of Oz." He later accepted, most magnanimously, our decision to create a history of the whole Oz phenomenon, leading up to the Disney production *Return to Oz*, rather than the "book of the film." Little did we realize, when we began our research, the extent and depth of this fascinating and fantastic subject. However, the perceptive professionalism of author Allen Eyles, combined with the strong contributions of researcher Mary Flower (in the United States), designer Roger Huggett and our editorial team, led by Charlotte Parry-Crooke and including Mike Darton and Talia Rodgers, has created a publication that we believe is a splendid introduction to the eternally exciting subject of Oz.

It must be said that, apart from renowned Oz expert Justin Schiller in New York, much of the Oz "establishment" has remained somewhat bemused by the commitment of an English publishing house to this subject. However, the cooperation of numerous American museums and libraries and the Archives of Walt Disney Productions, and the availability of the remarkable material contained in the original Baum books (including some of the finest graphics of the last 80 years), have enabled us to reveal the history of one of the greatest literary fantasies of all time.

My special thanks go to Walter Murch for his assistance and interest in this book – and his foreword to it. There are few film directors as sympathetically close to the Oz subject. Walt Disney Productions, especially Wendall Mohler, Wayne Morris and Dave Smith, and Gary Kurtz have been extremely helpful with material from their film *Return to Oz*. And we thank our co-publishers for their commitment and support. Finally, as Oz enthusiasts ourselves, we hope this book, and the 1985 Disney film, *Return to Oz*, will encourage many to read or reread the remarkable Baum books and find themselves once again "somewhere over the rainbow."

Justin Knowles

Author's Acknowledgments

Many people helped "ease me on down the road" to completing this book in time. Particular thanks to Justin Case, Mark Everett, Barry Fishman, Veronica Hitchcock and (once again) Tom Vallance for their prompt and generous assistance; to Walter Murch and Gary Kurtz at Elstree Studios who helped with coverage of their own film, Walt Disney's *Return to Oz* and with the project as a whole, and to their assistants Glynis Robertson and Sue Matthews for conscientiously attending to the details; to the British Film Institute for viewing facilities (Jackie Morris, Pete Flower, Nicki North, Jim Adams) and for locating illustrations (Michelle Snapes, Elaine Crowther); to Philip Dampier and Odyssey Video for the loan of their *Return to Oz* (the animated version); and to Joel W. Finler. Special thanks also for the unusual encouragement extended by the editorial department of the Justin Knowles organization – from Charlotte Parry-Crooke and Talia Rodgers to the renowned JK himself.

This book is for my daughter, Michelle.

CONTENTS

FOREWORD

Dorothy (played by Fairuza Balk) travels the Yellow Brick Road in *Return to Oz* (1985). Inset: Walter Murch, co-writer and director of *Return to Oz,* shown during production with Billina the Hen. [© Walt Disney Productions. Photographed by Barry Peake.]

The Chicago World's Fair of 1893 — a celebration of the 400th anniversary of the discovery of America — was a gleaming, electrified "White City" built around a series of artificial lagoons along the shore of Lake Michigan. At least 25 million people (one out of every four Americans living at the time) visited the fair in the months it was open to the public. One of these visitors was Lyman Frank Baum, 37, who had recently arrived with his family from the Dakota Territories. The farming boom of the 1870s and 1880s was over, and the newspaper he had founded, and the general store he had opened, had both gone under in the first years of the depression of the 1890s.

The contrast between the "great gray prairie" and acre upon acre of marvelous neoclassical exhibition halls, filled with happy people gazing at fantastic new inventions, must have left its mark upon Baum. Similar awe must have been felt by the hundreds of thousands of farmers and their families who were forced, like Baum, to leave their homesteads and find a new life in the cities of the Midwest during the following decade.

The burgeoning optimism about the future of cities and their civilizing influence in that era is hard to imagine today. Yet it fueled a generation of idealistic civic works that still can be seen in cities throughout the Midwest.

In L. Frank Baum it sparked a work of children's literature — *The Wizard of Oz*, published in 1900 — that has left indelible images on almost a century of readers and film-goers: Dorothy Gale's gray Kansas farm; the tornado that picks her up and deposits her in the land of Oz; the yellow-brick road leading to the Emerald City. These places, and the characters Baum invented to fill them, seem by now so autonomous that it is strange to think that they all emerged, as all great art does, from a specific time and set of circumstances to become the first, and perhaps only, authentically American fairy tale. And yet, like all great art, it transcends the circumstances of its birth. Four generations later, *The Wizard of Oz* is immediately accessible to readers all over the world.

I was introduced to Baum's work very early in life by my mother, who had avidly read the Oz books as a young girl in Ceylon. The daughter of a missionary, she was born in Ceylon and did not see America until the family returned just before World War I.

In some way, I suspect the Oz books, relating the story of a young girl's trip to a fabulous faraway land, became mixed in her mind with the voyage she would one day take back "home." In any case, the books made a deep impression on her, and she made sure I got to know them as soon as I was able to read. In fact, *Ozma of Oz*, which is partly the basis for the film *Return to Oz*, is the first "real" book I remember reading by myself.

After publication of *The Wizard of Oz*, Baum wrote 13 other stories about Oz — nearly a book a year until his death in 1919. In them, he originated hundreds of fantastic new characters and situations, a number of which were included in Walt Disney's *Return to Oz*. I hope this book — and the film — are enjoyable and that they serve to intrigue another generation of readers to follow Dorothy along Baum's yellow-brick road into his world of Oz.

Walter Murch
Director of *Return to Oz*
London 1985

INTRODUCTION

"Somewhere, over the rainbow," there may be people who have never heard of Dorothy, the Scarecrow, the Tin Woodman, the Cowardly Lion or the Wizard of Oz.

But it seems unlikely.

The 1939 film *The Wizard of Oz* is now considered to be the most popular film of all time. It is estimated to have been watched at least a billion times, largely through its repeated television screenings. Single showings on American television have at times attracted 50 million viewers.

The Wizard of Oz is also high on the list of the top-selling book titles of the 20th century. First published in 1900, the book has sold well over 7 million copies in numerous editions.

The appeal of the book, and more especially the film, extends to many countries. The book appeared in Great Britain almost immediately following its American publication and has been a steady favorite since then. The book has also been translated into about 30 foreign languages. Many European readers have "followed the yellow brick road" in Germany, Holland, Italy, Portugal, Spain and Sweden. The story has been popular in China, Japan and Taiwan. It is also well-known in Hungary, Poland, Rumania and especially the Soviet Union.

Acknowledged an international classic, the film's appeal is undiminishing. In six Christmas broadcasts on British television since 1975, it has accumulated a total estimated audience of 80 million — more than the country's entire population. These statistics point out its widespread appeal and repeated viewings, an indication of widespread affection for the film.

Stage versions are almost as old as the book itself. Since 1939, many have been based on the film and its songs. In the 1970s the original story gave birth to a black musical, *The Wiz*, that is still performed.

But there is much more to the story of Oz than just a book and film. Even in the United States it is little known that L. Frank Baum, author of *The Wizard of Oz*, wrote 13 subsequent Oz books, and other writers followed with more.

Now there is a spectacular new adventure movie from the Disney Studio, *Return to Oz*, based on some of the later stories. At last the public will be able to enjoy more of the wonderful imagination of Baum. Now viewers can begin to appreciate the full extent of the World of Oz.

Toto, the Scarecrow and Dorothy (played by Toto, Ray Bolger and Judy Garland) in the 1939 film *The Wizard of Oz*. [© 1939 Loew's Incorporated. Copyright renewed 1966 by Metro-Goldwyn-Mayer, Inc.]

PROFILES FROM THE LAND OF OZ

First, a flavor of the World of Oz as created by L. Frank Baum. Then the story of how it came about.

We profile most of the major figures who are featured regularly in the Baum books. They are preceded by a broad description of the amazing Land itself. The characters are arranged in the order in which they appear in the books. The first seven profiles concern characters world-renowned from the 1939 film, *The Wizard of Oz*; others have now achieved similar recognition in the new Disney production, *Return to Oz*.

Here, the characters are described according to Baum's text and shown as they were depicted by the illustrators at the time. We also include some later representations of these characters to indicate how faithfully (or otherwise) Baum's conceptions were followed.

The Land and Its People

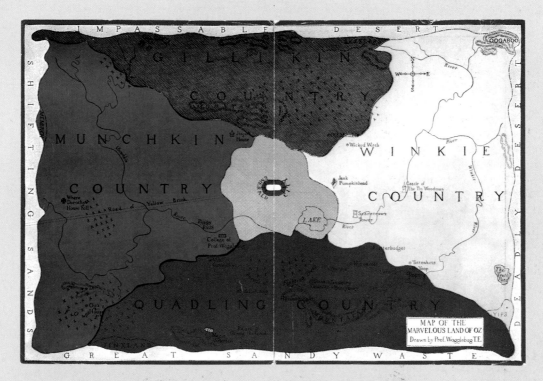

MAP OF THE MARVELOUS LAND OF OZ
Drawn by Prof. Wogglebug T.E.

Professor Woggle-Bug's map first appeared as an end-paper to the 1914 Oz tale, *Tik-Tok of Oz*. The Professor originally located Munchkin Country in the west of Oz, and Winkie Country in the east, reversing the positions most often given them in the Oz books. An attempt was made to correct the map by simply switching the compass directions for east and west.

[Courtesy of Contemporary Books Inc., Chicago.]

Oz is a rectangular country of contrasting colors. It is divided into four parts. The North contains the purple Gillikin country. The East is the blue Munchkin country. In the South lies the red land of the Quadlings. The West is the pleasant yellow country of the Winkies. In the center of Oz is the Emerald City, and in its green palace lives Ozma, the Fairy Princess and ruler of Oz.

Oz was no different from anywhere else until the Fairy Queen Lurline flew over with her group and left her daughter, Ozma, to rule. From that day, no one among the half-million population has grown any older, become sick, or died. Mortals entering Oz from outside, like Dorothy, also stop aging while they are there. All birds and beasts, as well as most fish, can talk in the Land of Oz.

Money is not used, and people work only half the time. Everything belongs to Ozma, and everyone shares what they have. "Our Land of Oz is a Land of love, and here friendship outranks every other quality," declares Ozma.

The Tin Woodman sums it up: "The people of Oz have but one law to obey, which is 'Behave yourself'." No army is needed and the people are happy in their beautiful country.

But . . . .

Witches, magicians and sorcerers still practice their skills in outlying parts of Oz. There are dangerous wild creatures in some places. There are also natural hazards, such as the road that slides back, the river that reverses, trees that seize people and mountains that twirl around. There are remote people who fight among themselves, who have never heard of Ozma and who are not impressed when they do. And there are external threats to Oz, mainly through the machinations of the Nome King who lives beneath the ground of the neighboring land of Ev.

Altogether, there is enough variety and drama in Oz to fill 14 books of highly imaginative stories by the original author, and then many more by others.

Dorothy and Toto

Dorothy Gale is an orphan girl who literally blows into Oz from Kansas with her dog, Toto. She becomes a treasured friend of its ruler, Ozma, who makes her a Princess of Oz. Dorothy later uses a magic belt to help protect her from harm in fairyland.

She makes her first return to Oz in *Ozma of Oz* after adventures with the Nome King. Later, another visit occurs by accident, when the buggy in which she is riding falls into a crack in the ground caused by an earthquake [*Dorothy and the Wizard in Oz*]. She finds herself again on the way to Oz in *The Road to Oz* when the roads near her farm are deliberately mixed up to bring her back. In *The Emerald City of Oz*, Dorothy signals Ozma to bring her to Oz and gains permission to have her Aunt Em and Uncle Henry live there with her permanently.

Toto is "a little black dog, with long, silky hair and small black eyes" who is Dorothy's faithful companion. For a long time it seems that he is an exception to the rule that animals can speak in the Land of Oz. He understands what is said to him, and barks and wags his tail in answer. Finally, in *Tik-Tok of Oz*, he reveals he can talk after all!

The plump Dorothy drawn by W. W. Denslow for *The Wizard of Oz* (1900), seen with Toto and the Scarecrow, and Dorothy as depicted in later Oz books by John R. Neill (from *The Patchwork Girl of Oz*, 1913). [Latter: courtesy of Contemporary Books Inc., Chicago.]

Dorothy turned brunette on film. Top: Judy Garland with Toto in *The Wizard of Oz* (1939). Far left: Dorothy Dwan in *The Wizard of Oz* (1925). Left: Diana Ross cradling Toto in *The Wiz* (1978). [Top: © 1939 Loew's Incorporated. Copyright renewed 1966 by Metro-Goldwyn-Mayer, Inc. Far left: courtesy of National Film Archive, London. Left: courtesy of National Film Archive, London — copyright © by Universal Pictures.]

Below: Toto by Denslow from *The Wizard of Oz* (1900).

The Scarecrow

Right: the Scarecrow as first encountered by Dorothy in *The Wizard of Oz* (1900). Illustration by W.W. Denslow. Below: as portrayed by Ray Bolger with Judy Garland as Dorothy in the 1939 film *The Wizard of Oz*. Below center: Michael Jackson in the film of the black musical version of the story, *The Wiz* (1978). Below right: the Scarecrow (Justin Case) being crowned by Dorothy (Fairuza Balk) in *Return to Oz* (1985).

[Below: © 1939 Loew's Incorporated. Copyright renewed 1966 by Metro-Goldwyn-Mayer, Inc. Below center: courtesy of National Film Archive, London — copyright © by Universal Pictures. Below right: © Walt Disney Productions.]

The most popular and beloved figure in all the land of Oz is a "man" of straw brought to life. Described in *The Tin Woodman of Oz*, ". . . the Scarecrow's body was only a suit of clothes filled with straw. The coat was buttoned tight to keep the packed straw from falling out and a rope was tied around the waist to hold it in shape and prevent the straw from sagging down. The Scarecrow's head was a gunnysack filled with bran, on which the eyes, nose and mouth had been painted. His hands were white cotton gloves stuffed with fine straw. . . . Even when carefully stuffed and patted into shape, the straw man was awkward in his movements and decidedly wobbly on his feet."

Able literally to have all the stuffing knocked out of him, he has only to be refilled with any suitable material to come back to life. His brains are "the Carefully-Assorted, Double-Distilled, High-Efficiency sort that the Wizard of Oz makes." But he is vulnerable to fire and spoiling by water. From time to time he has his face re-painted by the girl named Jinjur. One painted eye is usually larger than the other.

He has no need to rest, eat or sleep, and he enjoys passing the time with the

Tin Woodman. Referring to their friends of flesh and blood, he comments on the fact that "Meat tires, after a day's travel, while straw and tin never tire at all. Which proves that we are somewhat superior to people made in the common way."

After ruling Oz until Ozma appears to take her rightful place, he stays on at the Emerald City. Finally, though, his yearning for the countryside becomes too great, and he builds himself a corncob castle in Winkie country.

Left: as depicted by John R. Neill (from *The Scarecrow of Oz,* 1915). Below left: Frank Moore as the Scarecrow in L. Frank Baum's own film production of *His Majesty, the Scarecrow of Oz* (1914). Below: Larry Semon in the 1925 movie of *The Wizard of Oz.* [Left: courtesy of Contemporary Books Inc., Chicago. Below left: courtesy of Em Gee Film Library. Below: courtesy of National Film Archive, London.]

The Tin Woodman

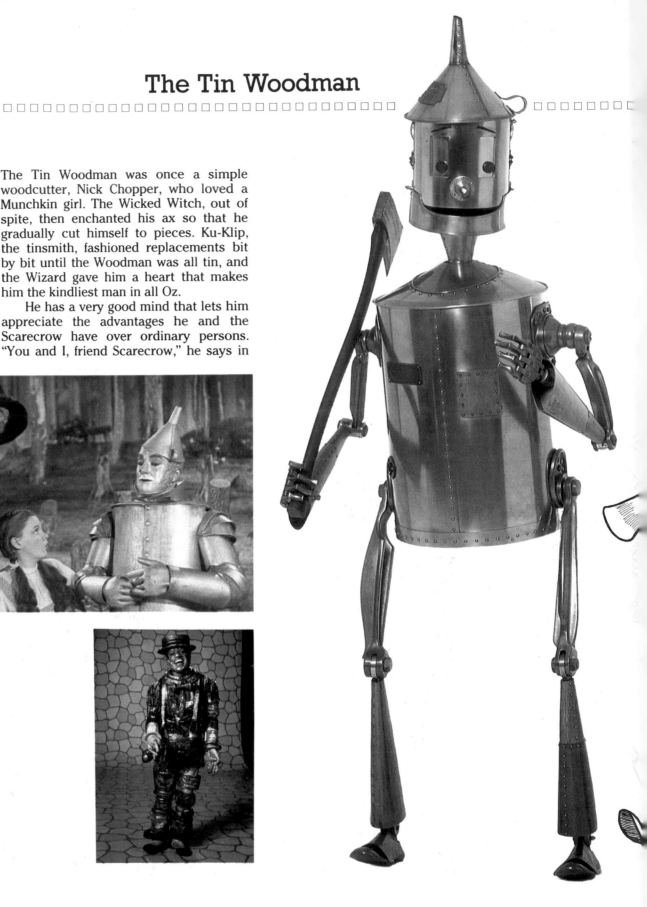

The Tin Woodman was once a simple woodcutter, Nick Chopper, who loved a Munchkin girl. The Wicked Witch, out of spite, then enchanted his ax so that he gradually cut himself to pieces. Ku-Klip, the tinsmith, fashioned replacements bit by bit until the Woodman was all tin, and the Wizard gave him a heart that makes him the kindliest man in all Oz.

He has a very good mind that lets him appreciate the advantages he and the Scarecrow have over ordinary persons. "You and I, friend Scarecrow," he says in

Above: the Tin Woodman as portrayed by Jack Haley in the 1939 movie of *The Wizard of Oz*, with the Scarecrow (Ray Bolger) and Dorothy (Judy Garland). Right: Nipsey Russell in *The Wiz* (1978). Far right: as re-created in the tradition of the John R. Neill illustrations for *Return to Oz* (1985). [Above: © 1939 Loew's Incorporated. Copyright renewed 1966 by Metro-Goldwyn-Mayer, Inc. Right: courtesy of National Film Archive, London — copyright © by Universal Pictures. Far right: © Walt Disney Productions.]

The Lost Princess of Oz, "are much more easily cared for than those clumsy meat people, who spend half their time dressing in fine clothes and who must live in splendid dwellings in order to be contented and happy. You and I do not eat, and so we are spared the dreadful bother of getting three meals a day. Nor do we waste half our lives in sleep, a condition that causes the meat people to lose all consciousness and become as thoughtless and helpless as logs of wood." The Tin Woodman must keep the dew off his body if he stays out at night, or he might rust solid. He is never without his gleaming, sharp ax.

He becomes Emperor of the Winkies after the Wicked Witch is destroyed by Dorothy in the falling house, but his authority is purely nominal. He lives in a magnificent Tin Castle in which the furniture, floors and walls are made of tin. There, he is attended by servants in tin uniforms who gave him a weekly polish and oil his joints. Sometimes the Winkies form an orchestra to play numbers like *The Shining Emperor Waltz* on their tin instruments. His gardens are full of tin flowers surrounded by tin birds that are wound up daily so they move and chirp.

The Tin Woodman as drawn by John R. Neill (left: from *The Land of Oz*, 1904) and by W. W. Denslow (in *The Wizard of Oz*, 1900). Frame enlargement of Pierre Couderc as the Tin Woodman in the 1914 film *His Majesty, the Scarecrow of Oz* (left), and (below) David Montgomery in the 1902 Chicago stage production of *The Wizard of Oz* with Anna Laughlin as Dorothy.

[Frame enlargement courtesy of Em Gee Film Library. Stage picture courtesy of Performing Arts Research Center, The New York Public Library at Lincoln Center.]

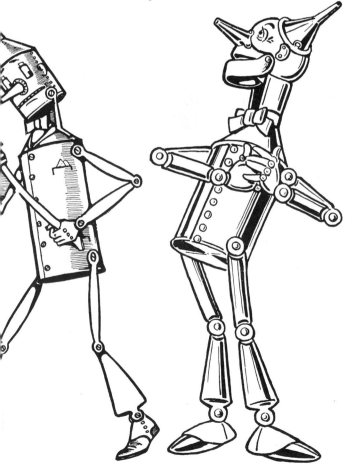

The Cowardly Lion

"The most important and intelligent beast in all Oz," the Cowardly Lion becomes one of the protectors of its ruler, Ozma, and helps draw her chariot when she visits the land of Ev in *Ozma of Oz*.

He is as big as a small horse but bursts into tears when Dorothy slaps his face at their first meeting. "All the other animals in the forest naturally expect me to be brave, for the Lion is everywhere thought to be the King of Beasts. I learned that if I roared very loudly every living thing was frightened and got out of my way. Whenever I've met a man I've been awfully scared; but I just roared at him, and he has always run away as fast as he could go. If the elephants and the tigers and the bears had ever tried to fight me, I should have run myself — I'm such a coward," he explains to her in *The Wizard of Oz*.

But, as is mentioned much later (in *Glinda of Oz*), "all who knew him knew that the Cowardly Lion's fears were coupled with bravery and that however much he might be frightened he summoned courage to meet every danger he encountered. Often he had saved Dorothy and Ozma in times of peril, but afterward he moaned and trembled and wept because he had been so scared."

The tawny creature is particularly friendly with the Hungry Tiger, with whom he shares the difficulty of refraining from eating other living creatures in accordance with the rules of good behavior in Oz.

The Wizard

The Wizard's real name is Oscar Zoroaster Diggs, and he was born in Omaha. Nicknamed Oz, he ran away as a young man to join a circus and became a ventriloquist and hot-air balloonist called the Wizard. One flight brought him to Oz, where the name "OZ" emblazoned on the side of his balloon caused him to be proclaimed the new Wizard.

It was he who built the Emerald City in the middle of Oz, hoping the Wicked Witches would leave him alone and not learn he was a fake wizard, a humbug. He arranged for the witch Mombi to hide the real heir to the throne, Ozma. Fortunately for him, that is forgotten when Ozma is restored to her rightful place and appoints him "Official Wizard."

He is a wizened little old man who dresses in black. "The Wizard wasn't exactly handsome but he was pleasant to look at. His bald head was as shiny as if it had been varnished; there was always a merry twinkle in his eyes and he was as spry as a schoolboy." From the Good Witch Glinda he learns real tricks of magic. The two of them become the only ones officially permitted to practice magic for the benefit of all the inhabitants of Oz.

Left: W. W. Denslow's depiction of the Wizard exposed as a humbug but unrepentant, in *The Wizard of Oz* (1900). Right: John R. Neill's warmer concept of the Wizard, taken from *The Patchwork Girl of Oz* (1913). [Latter: courtesy of Contemporary Books Inc., Chicago.]

Top: Frank Morgan as *The Wizard of Oz* (1939). Above: marionette of the Wizard from Bil Baird's 1968 New York puppet production, *The Wizard of Oz*. [Top: © 1939 Loew's Incorporated. Copyright renewed 1966 by Metro-Goldwyn-Mayer, Inc. Above: courtesy of Bil Baird.]

Glinda

The Good Witch and Official Sorceress of the Kingdom of Oz, Glinda is the most valued servant of the ruler, Ozma. She lives in a splendid palace built of rare marble at the southernmost edge of Oz in Quadling country. There, she presides over the Quadlings from her throne of rubies, attended by a hundred beautiful maids of honor. She travels around Oz in a chariot drawn by storks.

"No one knows her age, but all can see how beautiful and stately she is. Her hair is like red gold and finer than the finest silken strands. Her eyes are blue as the sky and always frank and smiling. Her cheeks are the envy of peach-blows and her mouth is as enticing as a rosebud. Glinda is tall and wears splendid gowns that trail behind her as she walks. She wears no jewels, for her beauty would shame them."

In Glinda's palace is the Great Book of Records, which notes everything that takes place everywhere in the world as it happens. Scanning it, she is often able to help others when she reads of evil deeds. She is the most powerful practitioner of magic in the Land of Oz and turns the humbug Wizard into a real one by teaching him how to use spells.

Jack Pumpkinhead

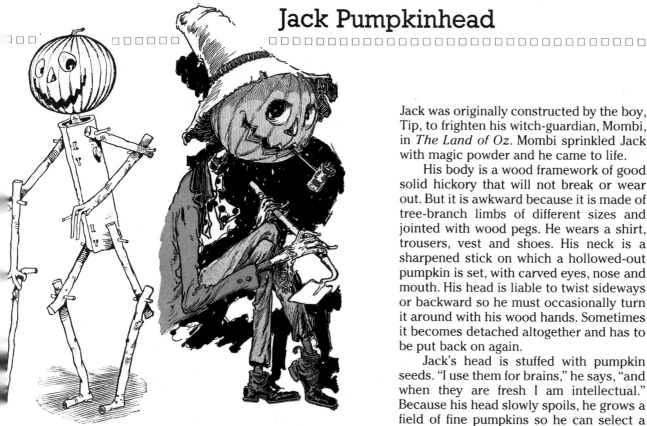

Three John R. Neill illustrations showing Jack Pumpkinhead. Above: from *The Land of Oz* (1904). Above right: from *The Patchwork Girl of Oz* (1913). Right: at home in *The Road to Oz* (1909). Far right: the character as he appears in *Return to Oz* (1985). [Last: © Walt Disney Productions.]

Jack was originally constructed by the boy, Tip, to frighten his witch-guardian, Mombi, in *The Land of Oz*. Mombi sprinkled Jack with magic powder and he came to life.

His body is a wood framework of good solid hickory that will not break or wear out. But it is awkward because it is made of tree-branch limbs of different sizes and jointed with wood pegs. He wears a shirt, trousers, vest and shoes. His neck is a sharpened stick on which a hollowed-out pumpkin is set, with carved eyes, nose and mouth. His head is liable to twist sideways or backward so he must occasionally turn it around with his wood hands. Sometimes it becomes detached altogether and has to be put back on again.

Jack's head is stuffed with pumpkin seeds. "I use them for brains," he says, "and when they are fresh I am intellectual." Because his head slowly spoils, he grows a field of fine pumpkins so he can select a new one when necessary. He then takes off his old head and uses it as a guide to carve a new face. Although his face is always set in a perpetual grin "as if its wearer considered life the jolliest thing imaginable," some of his faces are more cheerful than others. Because he is the only living pumpkinhead figure in Oz, it is always clear who he is. He keeps a graveyard of his discarded heads and lives in a huge pumpkin with doors and windows cut out of it.

The Wooden Saw-Horse

"It had been rudely made, in the beginning, to saw logs upon, so that its body was a short length of a log, and its legs were stout branches fitted into four holes made in the body. The tail was formed by a small branch that had been left on the log, while the head was a gnarled bump on one end of the body. Two knots of wood formed the eyes, and the mouth was a gash chopped in the log. When the Saw-Horse first came to life it had no ears at all, and so could not hear; but the boy who then owned him had whittled two ears out of bark and stuck them in the head, after which the Saw-Horse heard very distinctly."

The Saw-Horse can talk, like every other creature in Oz, but prefers not to — unless asked a question. He never tires and is as fast as the wind. It is easy for him to beat Jim the Cab-Horse, an animal of flesh and blood, when challenged to a race in *Dorothy and the Wizard in Oz*. He never needs to wear a bridle or reins because he responds to spoken instructions and is a great favorite of Ozma's. She had the ends of his wood legs shod with gold to keep them from wearing out. He lives in the stables at her Royal Palace in the Emerald City, and he has a saddle glittering with jewels. Occasionally, he draws the Royal Red Wagon, a vehicle inlaid with rubies and pearls that is almost a chariot.

Above: the Wooden Saw-Horse draws the Red Wagon with Ozma, Dorothy and Toto aboard in this Neill illustration from *The Tin Woodman of Oz* (1918). Right: Neill drawing from *The Land of Oz* (1904). [Former: courtesy of Contemporary Books Inc., Chicago.]

The Woggle-Bug

The leading pedant of Oz, H.M. Professor Woggle-Bug T.E., is described in *The Land of Oz* as having "a great, round, bug-like body supported upon two slender legs which ended in delicate feet — the toes curling upward. The body of the Woggle-Bug was rather flat, and judging from what could be seen of it was of a glistening dark brown color upon the back, while the front was striped with alternate bands of light brown and white, blending together at the edges. Its arms were fully as slender as its legs, and upon a rather long neck was perched its head — not unlike the head of a man, except that its nose ended in a curling antenna, or 'feeler,' and its ears from the upper points bore antennae that decorated the sides of its head like two miniature, curling pig tails. It must be admitted that the round, black eyes were rather bulging in appearance; but the expression on the Woggle-Bug's face was by no means unpleasant.

"For dress the insect wore a dark-blue swallow-tail coat with a yellow silk lining and a flower in the button-hole; a vest of white duck that stretched tightly across the wide body; knickerbockers of fawn-colored plush, fastened at the knees with gilt buckles; and, perched upon its small

head, was jauntily set a tall silk hat."

The Woggle-Bug is thoroughly educated (T.E.) and highly magnified (H.M.), having escaped from a school while under the magnifying-glass. He becomes the Public Educator of Oz and President of the Royal College of Art and Athletic Perfection. There, his invention of easily-swallowed sugar-coated tablets of learning enables the students to absorb their lessons painlessly. They can then devote all their time to games. However, his invention of square-meal tablets to save eating is not as well received by the students.

Above: the Woggle-Bug makes his debut in the Oz saga in *The Land of Oz* (1904) to the surprise of Jack Pumpkinhead, the Tin Woodman, the Scarecrow and a boy named Tip.

Ozma

The daughter of Queen Lurline, Ozma was left to rule Oz. Although she looks 14 or 15 years old, she is of course older because no one ages in this fairyland. She is the benevolent, but powerful, ruler of Oz and is even more beautiful than Glinda.

"She is said to be the most beautiful girl the world has ever known, and her heart and mind are as lovely as her person." (*The Emerald City of Oz.*)

"Merely to see her is to love her for her charming face and manners; to know her is to love her for her tender sympathy, her generous nature, her truth and honor. Born of a long line of Fairy Queens, Ozma is as nearly perfect as any fairy may be, and she is noted for her wisdom as well as for her other qualities. Her happy subjects adore their girl Ruler and each one considers her a comrade and protector." (*The Scarecrow of Oz.*)

Although Ozma is very friendly with

24

Billina

her girl visitors, Dorothy, and in later stories Trot and Betsy Bobbin, she is always quite aware of her position. She maintains "a certain reserve that lent her dignity in her most joyous moods." Ozma keeps an eye on her subjects' welfare with her magic picture, in which she can see what is happening anywhere in the world at that moment. She also has certain magic powers in the silver wand she carries. In particular, she tolerates no nonsense from people in more remote areas of Oz who have never heard of her and are reluctant to acknowledge her as their ruler.

She was originally the only yellow chicken in her whole farmyard brood and had the name "Bill" given to her. On board a ship bound for Australia (in *Ozma of Oz*), her coop was washed overboard in a storm, and she drifted on the ocean with Dorothy. There, she found to her amazement that she could talk. Dorothy promptly renamed her Billina.

She is lively, intelligent and talkative, and accompanies Dorothy when they reach fairyland. Together they enter the underground world of the Nomes. Hiding under his throne she overhears the Nome King's secret, which is that eggs terrify him and his people. It is also the quick-witted Billina who prompts Dorothy to grab the Nome King's magic belt and render him powerless.

Later on, Billina hatches 10 fluffy chicks. Because she can't tell them apart, she calls them all Dorothy and has each chick wear a tiny gold chain holding a locket with the letter "D" engraved on the outside. Inside each locket is a picture of her good friend Dorothy. In time, Billina hatches thousands of chicks in the Land of Oz.

Left: Billina with Dorothy in the 1985 movie, *Return to Oz*. Center and right: two illustrations by John R. Neill from *Ozma of Oz* (1907), one showing her with Dorothy. [Left: © Walt Disney Productions.]

Tik-Tok

Dorothy discovered this clockwork robot in a chamber cut in rock in Wheeler country outside Oz. "He was only about as tall as Dorothy herself, and his body was round as a ball and made out of burnished copper. Also his head and limbs were copper, and these were jointed or hinged to his body in a peculiar way, with metal caps over the joints, like the armor worn by knights in days of old." (*Ozma of Oz.*)

Tik-Tok explains his name in his mechanical, expressionless way of speaking. "My for-mer ma-ster gave me that name be-cause my clock-work al-ways ticks when it is wound up." Tik-Tok is very reliable because he does what he is told. But he becomes helpless when his machinery runs down and is easily immobilized by falling over.

He is fortunate not to have feelings. In the book named for him, *Tik-Tok of Oz*, he is thrown down a well. Then, falling down a tube through the center of the Earth, he ends up in a marble fountain filled with water on the other side.

Right: the copper machine man walks to freedom from the rocky cavern in *Ozma of Oz* (1907) watched by Dorothy and Billina. Left: Neill's illustrations provide the key for re-creating Tik-Tok in the 1985 movie, *Return to Oz*. [Latter: © Walt Disney Productions.]

SMITH & TINKER'S

Patent Double-Action, Extra-Responsive,
Thought-Creating, Perfect-Talking

MECHANICAL MAN

Fitted with our Special Clock-Work Attachment.

Thinks, Speaks, Acts, and Does Everything but Live.

Manufactured only at our Works at Evna, Land of Ev.
All infringements will be promptly Prosecuted according to Law.

DIRECTIONS FOR USING:

For THINKING:—Wind the Clock-work Man under his left arm, (marked No. 1.)

For SPEAKING:—Wind the Clock-work Man under his right arm, (marked No. 2.)

For WALKING and ACTION:—Wind Clock-work in the middle of his back, (marked No. 3.)

N. B.—This Mechanism is guaranteed to work perfectly for a thousand years.

The Nome King

The Nomes are sprites who dwell underneath the land of Ev, which is separated by a deadly desert from Oz. Their king is Roquat the Red, or Ruggedo, and he is the principal villain of the Oz stories. "The Monarch of all the Metals and Precious Stones of the Underground World was a round little man with a flowing white beard, a red face, bright eyes and a scowl that covered all his forehead."

Ranting and roaring, he makes life miserable for everyone around him. His jewel-studded belt possesses certain magical powers useful to him — until Dorothy takes it away from him. Because he believes all metals now on the earth's surface were once part of his subterranean kingdom, he hates all earth-crawlers who dig up metals. He resents anybody having "his" metals.

Roquat greatly fears Dorothy. "She insists on the Nomes being goody-goody, which is contrary to their natures. Dorothy gets angry if I do the least thing that is wicked, and tries to make me stop it, and that naturally makes me down-hearted," he complains in *Rinkitink in Oz*.

Like all Nomes, he is immortal unless he comes into contact with an egg. "Eggs belong to the outside world — to the world on the earth's surface . . . Here, in my underground kingdom, they are rank poison . . . and we Nomes can't bear them around," he says in *Ozma of Oz*.

When stripped of power, and exiled, the Nome King still never for long loses his thirst to conquer Oz.

Above: the Nome King with Dorothy and Ozma in a Neill illustration from *Ozma of Oz* (1907), and left: with Billina and one of her poisonous eggs in the same book. Far left: Nicol Williamson portrayed the Nome King in the 1985 movie, *Return to Oz*. [Last: © Walt Disney Productions.]

The Shaggy Man

Polychrome

"His clothes were shaggy, his boots were shaggy and full of holes, and his hair and whiskers were shaggy. But his smile was sweet and his eyes were kind." The Shaggy Man doesn't want a fortune but he does want to be loved, and he travels across the United States with a Love Magnet to induce affection from everyone he meets.

He becomes one of the few outsiders permitted to settle in Oz. There, he doesn't need the Love Magnet, so it is placed above the gates to the Emerald City. Ozma makes him feel welcome on his first visit to the Royal Palace by giving him a handsome apartment. Another gift is a fine set of new clothes with shags and bobtails attached to make him feel comfortable.

A tramp and an outcast in the real world, he becomes an important citizen of Oz. It is his skill with the telegraph, for instance, that permits any form of communication with Oz after it severs connections with the rest of the world. On one occasion he leaves Oz to search for his long-lost brother. Eventually, the brother is found in the Nome Kingdom, and both return to Oz.

Polychrome is the most reckless of the daughters of the Rainbow. A fairy with a merry, infectious laugh, she usually lives in the Cloud Palaces in the sky. Her greatest joy is to dance on the pretty rays of the Rainbow. Often she skips off the end to the ground and is left behind by her father. On earth, she sips the dew by moonlight for nourishment, and her magic is sometimes useful to the friends she makes.

Her first appearance in the Oz stories, in *The Road to Oz*, is memorable. "A little girl, radiant and beautiful, shapely as a fairy and exquisitely dressed, was dancing gracefully in the middle of the lonely road, whirling slowly this way and that, her dainty feet twinkling in sprightly fashion. She was clad in flowing, fluffy robes of soft material that reminded Dorothy of woven cobwebs, only it was colored in soft tintings of violet, rose, topaz, olive, azure, and white, mingled together most harmoniously in stripes which melted one into the other with soft blendings. Her hair was like spun gold and floated around her in a cloud, no strand being fastened or confined by either pin or ornament or ribbon."

John Neill depicts the Shaggy Man in the 1913 story, *The Patchwork Girl of Oz.* [Courtesy of Contemporary Books Inc., Chicago.]

Polychrome, as drawn by Neill in *The Road to Oz* (1909), and as portrayed by Cherie Hawkins in the Coronation scene of *Return to Oz* (1985). [Latter: © Walt Disney Productions.]

The Glass Cat

Bungle, a female cat, is the result of testing the magic Powder of Life. "The cat was of transparent glass, through which one could plainly see its ruby heart beating and its pink brains whirling around in the top of the head. The Glass Cat's eyes were emeralds; its fluffy tail was of spun glass and very beautiful. The ruby heart, while pretty to look at, was hard and cold and the Glass Cat's disposition was not pleasant at all times. It scorned to catch mice, did not eat, and was extremely lazy. If you complimented the remarkable cat on her beauty, she would be very friendly, for she loved admiration above everything. The pink brains were always working and their owner was indeed more intelligent than most common cats." (*Glinda of Oz.*)

reprisal, they dip her in slimy blue mud.

She becomes so disagreeable that the Wizard of Oz eventually makes her brains transparent. After that she becomes a well-behaved palace pet. Then, in some unrecorded development, her brains are turned pink again, and she is as vain and obnoxious as before.

Two representations of the Glass Cat by John R. Neill from *The Patchwork Girl of Oz* (1913). [Courtesy of Contemporary Books Inc., Chicago.]

The Glass Cat likes observers to watch her brains roll and tumble about. "I have the handsomest brains in the world. They're pink and you can see 'em work," she declares incessantly. She declines to eat mice because they would look silly inside her glass body. Selfish, sour-tempered and saucy, she constantly quarrels with Eureka, the pink kitten of the Emerald City who thinks her flesh is better than glass. Bungle is humiliatingly treated when she teases some monkeys. In

I HATE DIGNITY

Scraps, the Patchwork Girl, in a John R. Neill illustration from *The Patchwork Girl of Oz* (1913). [Courtesy of Contemporary Books Inc., Chicago.]

The Patchwork Girl

Commonly known as Scraps, the Patchwork Girl was created out of an old patchwork bed quilt stuffed with cotton padding. She was brought to life by the crooked magician Dr. Pipt to be an obedient servant girl for his wife Margolotte. Grains of Obedience, Amiability, Truth and Cleverness were mixed into a powder by Margolotte and inserted into her round ball of a head. Ojo the Munchkin boy secretly added other ingredients, including an extra dose of Cleverness, so her personality was not as docile and compliant as intended.

Scraps has two button eyes sown on her face. In *The Lost Princess of Oz*, we are told that "For hair she had a mass of brown yarn and to make a nose for her a part of the cloth had been pulled into the shape of a knob and tied with a string to hold it in place. Her mouth had been carefully made by cutting a slit in the proper place and lining it with red silk, adding two rows of pearls for teeth and a bit of red flannel for a tongue.

"In spite of this queer make-up, the Patchwork Girl was magically alive and had proved herself not the least jolly and agreeable of the many quaint characters who inhabit the astonishing Fairyland of Oz. Indeed, Scraps was a general favorite, although she was rather flighty and erratic and did and said many things that surprised her friends. She was seldom still, but loved to dance, to turn handsprings and somersaults, to climb trees and to indulge in many other active sports."

She has a head full of nonsense rhymes and is always making songs out of them.

The Patchwork Girl as made up for the Coronation scene of *Return to Oz* (1985).
[© Walt Disney Productions.]

The Woozy

The Woozy is a one-of-a-kind wild beast who has been fenced in by Munchkin farmers to keep him from eating their honeybees. He is so tough that nothing can harm him. When he is angry, his eyes can literally burn objects. Nothing makes him angrier than someone saying "Krizzle-Kroo" to him, although he can't remember why. Mistakenly, he believes he has a terrifying growl.

One of his favorite boasts is "When I promise anything you can depend on it, 'cause I'm square" — which is not much less than the exact truth. "The creature was all squares and flat surfaces and edges. Its head was an exact square, like one of the building-blocks a child plays with; therefore it had no ears, but heard sounds through two openings in the upper corners. Its nose, being in the center of a square surface, was flat, while the mouth was formed by the opening of the lower edge of the block.

"The body of the Woozy was much larger than its head, but was likewise block-shaped — being twice as long as it was wide and high. The tail was square and stubby and perfectly straight, and the four legs were made in the same way, each being four-sided. The animal was covered with a thick, smooth skin and had no hair at all except at the extreme end of its tail, where there grew exactly three stiff, stubby hairs. The beast was dark blue in color and his face was not fierce nor ferocious in expression but rather good-humored and droll." (*The Patchwork Girl of Oz.*)

The Woozy, as depicted by Neill in *The Patchwork Girl of Oz* (1913), below submitting to the attempt by the Patchwork Girl and a Munchkin boy named Ojo to wrest the three hairs from his tail. The hairs are part of the ingredients for a magical cure. The Glass Cat looks on. [Both courtesy of Contemporary Books Inc., Chicago.]

The Frogman

As a common frog, the Frogman was carried by a bird to the tableland of the Yips in a remote corner of Winkie country in Oz. There, he grew large in an enchanted pool. The Yips were so impressed by him that he became their adviser, even in matters he knew nothing about, and their leader in times of emergency.

"The Frogman's usual costume consisted of knee-britches made of yellow satin plush, with trimmings of gold braid and jeweled knee-buckles; a white satin vest with silver buttons in which were set solitaire rubies; a swallow-tailed coat of bright yellow; green stockings and red leather shoes turned up at the toes and having diamond buckles. He wore, when he walked out, a purple silk hat and carried a gold-headed cane. Over his eyes he wore great spectacles with gold rims, not because his eyes were bad but because the spectacles made him look wise, and so distinguished and gorgeous was his appearance that all the Yips were proud of him." (*The Lost Princess of Oz.*)

He is full of his own importance. "Every time I open my mouth, I am liable to say something important," he declares.

"It is fortunate your mouth is so very wide and opens so far, for otherwise all the wisdom might not be able to get out of it," replies a companion.

The Frogman decides to confer the benefit of his colossal wisdom on the rest of Oz. However, a dip in the Truth Pond later obliges him to admit to his own limitations.

The Frogman, from *The Lost Princess of Oz* (1917), and left: as recreated for the Coronation scene in the 1985 film, *Return to Oz.*
[Former: courtesy of Contemporary Books Inc., Chicago. Latter: © Walt Disney Productions.]

THE CREATION OF OZ

□□□□□□□□□□□□□□□□□□□□□□□□□□□ □□□□□□

Before Oz

When *The Wizard of Oz* first appeared in bookstores in September 1900, its author, L. Frank Baum, was 44 years old. It was Baum's second fictional book, although he had been fascinated by printing and journalism since his wealthy father had bought him a printing press for his birthday when he was a teenager. He had then produced his own magazines, filling them with his stories and poems.

Lyman Frank Baum was born on May 15, 1856, at Chittenango in upper New York state. His father had made a fortune in Pennsylvania oil. Though part of a large family, he was a solitary child and an avid reader. He was educated at home, except for two unhappy years spent at a local military academy. In addition to printing, he was also fascinated by chickens, and by the age of 19 he had become a breeder. At another time he longed for an acting career and bought his way into a traveling theater company.

Baum worked for his father as a salesman and as manager of some theaters that belonged to the family. He also wrote for a weekly newspaper. At the age of 25 he wrote, produced and acted in a play, *The Maid of Arran*, an Irish melodrama with song. The play had moderate success and was even briefly staged in New York. But Baum's next attempts at playwriting were unsuccessful.

During his tour with *The Maid of Arran*, Baum met Maud Gage, whose mother was a writer and leading suffragette. In 1882, he married Maud, and the first of their four sons was born the following year.

In 1886, his first book was published. Titled *The Book of the Hamburgs*, it was a guide to the mating, rearing, management and exhibiting of the Hamburg breed of chicken.

Baum then took over his father's chain of theaters, only to lose them to creditors as a result of poor supervision. He also took over the marketing of a petroleum

L. Frank Baum (1856–1919), a master storyteller who knew what Robert Louis Stevenson called "the particular crown and triumph of the artist not to be merely true, not simply to convince but to enchant."

lubricant, an operation which he inherited on the death of his father and an older brother, but this too failed.

Now with a wife and two sons to support, Baum tried his luck in the Dakota Territory where Maud's brother and sisters had settled. There, his attempts to run a store, then a local newspaper, met with failure when the boom that had opened up the area collapsed. In South Dakota, Maud gave birth to two more sons.

Baum's luck changed in 1891, when he moved to Chicago and prospered as a traveling salesman, selling china and glassware. His mother-in-law, Matilda, listened to the stories Baum told his sons at bedtime, and she urged him to write some of them down. The result was *Mother Goose in Prose*, which was published with some success in Chicago in 1897. Inside the copy he presented to his sister he wrote:

When I was young I longed to write a great novel that should win me fame. Now that I am getting old my first book is written to amuse children. For, aside from my evident inability to do anything 'great,' I have learned to regard fame as a will-o-the-wisp which, when caught, is not worth the possession; but to please a child is a sweet and lovely thing that warms one's heart and brings its own reward. I hope that my book will succeed in that way — that the children will like it.

W. W. Denslow (a crayon drawing by Frank Holme, taken from *The Baum Bugle*, Autumn 1975) and his title page for the very first Oz book showing its original longer title.

Baum then launched a trade magazine, called *The Show Window*, about the dressing of store windows to attract customers. It too was profitable.

He became a member of the Chicago Press Club, and it was at the Club that he first met Philadelphia-born W.W. Denslow, who was to become his collaborator. Denslow, who was the same age, had a reputation as an illustrator. He designed posters and book jackets. Denslow was touchy and temperamental, and he habitually wore a red vest, sported a walrus moustache and smoked a corncob pipe.

Baum and Denslow became partners

L. Frank Baum at his summer cottage on Lake Michigan where he typed out *The Wizard of Oz* in 1899 from a longhand MS reputedly written on hotel stationery, wrapping material and other scraps of paper. [Courtesy of National Film Archive, London.]

The Original Story

The 1939 film closely followed Baum's story. But deletions and other differences from the book may surprise those who are familiar with only the movie.

The book begins on the Kansas prairie and introduces Dorothy Gale, an orphan about 6 years old, who lives with her Aunt Em and Uncle Henry and plays with her dog, Toto. A cyclone blows up, and Dorothy delays taking shelter while she looks for Toto. The wind blows away the house with Dorothy and Toto inside. They gently land in a strange country inhabited by short people called Munchkins where the color blue abounds.

The house has crushed the Wicked Witch of the East and freed the Munchkins from bondage. The Good Witch of the North arrives, explains to Dorothy that she is in fairyland and gives the dead witch's silver slippers to the girl.

Wanting to return home to Kansas, Dorothy is advised to follow the yellow brick road and seek assistance from Oz, the great unseen wizard who rules the Emerald City in the center of the country. En route, she meets the Scarecrow, who winks at her and bids her good day. She frees him from his pole, and he accompanies her, hoping to obtain some brains from the great Oz. They meet up with the Tin Woodman in the forest. He has been immobile for more than a year since his joints rusted. The Tin Woodman explains how he was once a normal woodchopper who loved a Munchkin girl. His ax was enchanted by the Witch of the East so he continually cut pieces off himself. He had to be patched up bit by bit with replacements of shaped tin. Now made entirely of tin, he goes along with the pair, hoping Oz can give him a heart. Next, a lion menaces them, and Dorothy slaps its nose to save Toto from being bitten. The lion proves to be a big coward and joins the party, hoping to acquire courage from the Wizard.

to finance the publication of another children's work, *Father Goose, His Book.* The book was a collection of Baum's poems, with color illustrations by Denslow. It became the top-selling new book for children in 1899. Even though Denslow's drawings attracted more attention than Baum's poetry, Baum was suddenly in demand as an author.

For years Baum had been creating a long fairy tale in his head. He tried it out in bits and pieces on his children and their friends. Eventually, after the success of *Father Goose*, it was accepted for publication. Called *The Wonderful Wizard of Oz*, the book went on sale in September 1900. But it didn't do as well as *Father Goose*, despite the publisher's extravagant claims to have sold nearly 90,000 by the end of 1901. The real figure was a little over 20,000 copies. This was still good, but like the *Wizard of Oz* film, its real success was to be measured in the long term rather than the present. The publisher went bankrupt in 1902, after overextending himself.

For a 1903 reprint by another publisher, the title was changed to *The New Wizard of Oz*. However, after the MGM film version came out in 1939, publishers have generally followed its lead and called the book *The Wizard of Oz*, recognizing that it is the book's best-known title.

Dorothy receives an audience with the Great Oz in his Throne Room and is confronted by an enormous Head. A Denslow illustration from *The Wizard of Oz* (1900).

An armless Hammerhead sends the Scarecrow tumbling in this W. W. Denslow illustration from the original *The Wizard of Oz*.

The Cowardly Lion leaps across a chasm, carrying the others in turn on his back. They cross another chasm on a tree trunk chopped down by the Woodman and escape from two Kalidahs, "monstrous beasts with bodies like bears and heads like tigers."

The Woodman makes a raft to cross a river, but the Scarecrow is stranded, clinging to a pole in mid-stream after it sticks in the river bed. A stork obligingly carries the Scarecrow to the bank.

The aroma of a poppy field puts Dorothy, Toto and the Cowardly Lion to sleep. The Tin Woodman and Scarecrow are unaffected and carry Dorothy and Toto to safety. Later, the Tin Woodman saves the Queen of the Field Mice from a wildcat's jaws, so she summons thousands of mice to drag the heavier Lion from the poppy field.

Soon they reach the Emerald City, where they are required to put on spectacles so that they see everything as dazzling green. They eventually obtain individual audiences with the Wizard. He appears to them in different forms — as a giant head, a lovely lady, a terrible beast and a ball of fire. He demands of each that they kill the Wicked Witch of the West. Only then will he grant their requests.

Dorothy reluctantly agrees to try to carry out his demand. With the others, she is spotted by the Witch as they enter her domain.

Forty wolves attack them, but the wolves are chopped to death by the Tin Woodman. Forty crows follow, and the Scarecrow twists their necks. Forty stinging bees break their wings on the tin body of the Woodman and die. The Witch now dispatches her slaves, the Winkies, but one roar from the Cowardly Lion sends them all fleeing. As a last resort, the Witch uses a Golden Cap to call on the Winged Monkeys to carry the Lion and Dorothy (with Toto in her arms) into her castle. The Witch tries to trick Dorothy into parting with her silver slippers which have magical powers. Dorothy retaliates by throwing water on the Witch, not knowing it will make her melt away. After the Witch melts, the Winged Monkeys carry the group back to the Emerald City, explaining to Dorothy how they fell under the power of the Witch.

The Wizard turns out to be a little, old, baldheaded man who admits to being a fraud. But he satisfies the Scarecrow with some pins and needles in bran for a brain. He puts a silk heart filled with sawdust in the Tin Woodman's chest, and he gives the Lion a drink of courage from a green bottle. To take Dorothy back to Kansas, he suggests using the balloon that carried him to Oz years before. The Wizard appoints the Scarecrow to rule in his place, but he

Chapter VIII.
The Deadly Poppy Field.

accidentally leaves without Dorothy.

Dorothy sets out to ask help from Glinda, the Good Witch of the South, and her three friends accompany her. They are attacked by the Fighting Trees before they arrive in the Dainty China country, where china people live in a land made of china.

Farther on, the Lion knocks the head off a giant spider, and the liberated beasts of the forest appoint him their king. The travelers then meet the armless Hammerheads who use the flat tops of their heads to butt them away. Dorothy summons the Winged Monkeys with the Golden Cap to carry them into the land of the Quadlings where Glinda rules.

Glinda agrees to help Dorothy in exchange for the Golden Cap, and then uses the powers of the Cap to send the Scarecrow back to govern the Emerald

City, to send the Tin Woodman to rule the Winkies, and to send the Cowardly Lion to be King of the Forest. Glinda then reveals to Dorothy she could have gone home at any time by using the silver slippers. So Dorothy does use the slippers, and is reunited with her Aunt Em.

A Classic of Its Kind

L. Frank Baum's book is a classic of its kind because it makes a vivid appeal to the reader's imagination. Dorothy is an average, bright, but unremarkable girl who could be any young reader. There is a fantastic array of characters, each different from the last. And there is a variety of settings, including areas with different "color codings."

It was one thing to describe this in words. It was another to bring it alive visually without deviating from the text. Denslow rose masterfully to the challenge in his illustrations. Without using full color anywhere, he took individual colors and used them solidly and in line tints to correspond with the colors Baum had attributed to certain areas. Denslow made far more extensive use of color than was then the practice in children's books. His drawings have a bold humor and individual style that must have contributed greatly to the success of the book. His designs spread imaginatively into the margins of the page and behind the text. His chapter headings and openings are strikingly done. The way Denslow uses the border of the picture in full-page drawings for characters to sit on is delightful. Similarly pleasing is his *art-nouveau* use of the poppies with their extravagantly curving stems. He draws all the characters as larger-than-life and comically exaggerated. Denslow may perhaps be criticized for being a bit too frivolous and lighthearted, especially when compared with the work of later illustrators.

To anyone familiar with the 1939 film (which is discussed later), the book has some glaring weaknesses.

The first chapter is a careful description of Dorothy's drab life in Kansas. Everything is gray — the land, the grass, the house. "It was Toto that made Dorothy laugh, and saved her from growing as gray as her other surroundings," writes Baum. Thin, gaunt Aunt Em never smiles and is amazed that Dorothy can find anything to laugh at. We also learn that "Uncle Henry never laughed. He worked hard from morning till night and did not know what joy was."

Dorothy has Toto with her in the Land of Oz, so *why* does she want to go back to Kansas? The Scarecrow can't understand it. "That is because you have no brains," answers the girl. "No matter how dreary and gray our homes are, we people of flesh and blood would rather live there than in any other country, be it ever so beautiful. There is no place like home."

She says this before the more alarming incidents happen to her, just after meeting the Scarecrow. She makes good friends in Oz — but still wants to go back to Kansas, where no farmhands or other companions are mentioned. One reason she suggests is so Aunt Em does not have to buy a mourning dress on the assumption that Dorothy is dead.

Charming integration of text and illustration on the final page of the first edition of *The Wizard of Oz*.

Watched by their Queen and helped by the Tin Woodman and the Scarecrow, the army of mice drag the sleeping lion from the deadly poppy field. A double-page spread of text and illustration from *The Wizard of Oz* (1900).

It is significant, but inconsistent, that Aunt Em has become a friendly, loving figure when Dorothy returns at the end of the story, even if relief at her safe return is a partial explanation.

There is some structural awkwardness in the book. Some episodes are too long, and hold up the pace of the action. The King of the Winged Monkeys, for example, insists on telling a long, complicated story of how they became slaves to the owner of the Golden Cap. After the main adventure in conquering the Wicked Witch of the West, Dorothy and friends encounter unnecessary difficulties with the Fighting Trees and the Hammerheads. And the interlude with the china people, who neither help nor hinder them, is another anticlimax.

With a confidence born of the new century, Baum writes in his introduction to *The Wizard of Oz* that the traditional style of fairy tale is only of historical interest. "The time has come for a series of newer 'wonder tales' in which the stereotyped genie, dwarf and fairy are eliminated, together with all the horrible and blood-curdling incidents devised by their authors to point a fearsome moral to each tale."

His book, he says, was written "solely to please children of today. It aspires to be a modernized fairy tale, in which the wonderment and joy are retained and the heartaches and nightmares are left out." Perhaps this was a new form of Baum's old skill at salesmanship — to persuade parents to buy the book.

In fact, the book contains even more gruesome and frightening imagery than the film. The Tin Woodman wields his ax very effectively. ". . . As the wildcat ran by he gave it a quick blow that cut the beast's head clean off its body, and it rolled over at his feet in two pieces."

Elsewhere, "He seized his ax, which he had made very sharp, and as the leader of the wolves came on the Tin Woodman swung his arm and chopped the wolf's head from its body, so that it immediately died. As soon as he could raise his ax

of each mouse and the other end to the truck. Of course the truck was a thousand times bigger than any of the mice who were to draw it; but when all the mice had been harnessed they were able to pull it quite easily. Even the Scarecrow and the Tin Woodman could sit on it, and were drawn swiftly by their queer little horses to the place where the Lion lay asleep.

After a great deal of hard work, for the Lion was heavy, they managed to get him up on the truck. Then

another wolf came up, and he also fell under the sharp edge of the Tin Woodman's weapon. There were forty wolves, and forty times a wolf was killed; so that at last they all lay dead in a heap before the Woodman."

The Scarecrow is just as deadly. After the Witch orders the King Crow to "peck out [the travelers'] eyes and tear them to pieces," the Scarecrow "caught it by the head and twisted its neck until dead." And then "There were forty crows, and forty times the Scarecrow twisted a neck."

The Cowardly Lion disposes of the giant spider monster — "He knocked the

the Queen hurriedly gave her people the order to start, for she feared if the mice stayed among the poppies too long they also would fall asleep.

At first the little creatures, many though they were, could hardly stir the heavily loaded truck; but the Woodman and the Scarecrow both pushed from behind, and they got along better. Soon they rolled the Lion out of the poppy bed to the green fields, where he could breathe the sweet, fresh air again, instead of the poisonous scent of the flowers.

spider's head from its body. Jumping down, he watched it until the long legs stopped wiggling, when he knew it was quite dead."

These are extreme examples from what is often a terrifying, nightmarish story. In later books, there is less of this type of disturbing material. Baum introduces a rule that no living thing can possibly be killed in Oz except visiting mortals.

Unlike *Alice in Wonderland*, which probably inspired Baum to have a small girl as his central figure, or the 1939 film, Dorothy's adventures are not explained as

a dream. But Baum may have toyed with the idea. He describes Dorothy heading for the cyclone cellar.

"When she was halfway across the room there came a great shriek from the wind, and the house shook so hard that she lost her footing and sat down suddenly on the floor. A strange thing then happened. The house whirled around two or three times and rose slowly through the air. Dorothy felt as if she were going up in a balloon."

It is almost as if Dorothy has hit her head and is experiencing the sensation of losing consciousness. But then Baum specifically describes her falling fast asleep, and the house is still in the air hours later. Moreover, at the end of the book, he writes that Uncle Henry has had to build a new farmhouse to replace the old one the cyclone carried away.

Baum did not originally intend to write more Oz books. The silver slippers fall off Dorothy's feet while she is traveling home, so she has no means to get back to Oz. He and Denslow collaborated instead on another long fairy tale, *Dot and Tot in Merryland*. Published in 1901, it never had the success of *The Wizard of Oz*.

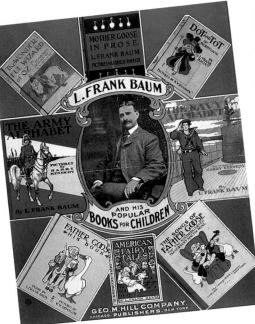

This 1901 publicity poster for the works of L. Frank Baum displays the covers of his other children's books as well as that of the first Oz tale. [Courtesy of the Chicago Historical Society.]

Part of the program and a poster for the 1903 New York stage production of *The Wizard of Oz* [Poster courtesy of Performing Arts Research Center, The New York Public Library at Lincoln Center.]

The First Stage Wizard

Between 1901 and 1902, Baum adapted *The Wizard of Oz* for the stage, providing the book and lyrics. A Chicago composer, Paul Tietjens, added the music, and Denslow designed the costumes and "scenic color effects".

Baum and Denslow had worked as partners on the book, and Denslow was not pleased at now finding he was to have a diminished role and financial interest in the stage production. They split up. Denslow drew some picture books that used the Oz characters as he had originally drawn them, but in new settings.

The stage play needed professional revision to make it comparable with other musical comedies of the time and to have it appeal to adult audiences. A small girl and a dog would have been impractical in any case, so Dorothy became a teenager who went to Oz with a pantomine cow named Imogene. She was given some romantic interest, in the form of an adoring poet named Sir Dashemoff Daily. A waitress, Tryxie Trifle, also blew in from Kansas, and a wicked nobleman, Sir Wiley Gyle, was added to the plot, along with the former King of Oz, Pastoria, who sought to recover his throne from the Wizard.

Numerous songs were introduced, some sung by chorus girls who formed the Army of Oz or who donned large hats to represent the poppies in a field. The sets were spectacular, especially the courtyard of the Wizard's palace. There were also some enthralling special effects, notably the cyclone and the snowfall that awakens the dozing Dorothy in the poppy field.

How much Baum participated in the revisions is not clear, but joke-writers were employed to help develop comedy routines for the Scarecrow and Tin Woodman. These characters, as played by the acting team of Fred Stone and David Montgomery, became the stars of the show. The plot of the play followed the story of the book, but it is Dorothy who wishes the Scarecrow to life with a magic

ring given her by the Good Witch as a reward for having killed the Wicked Witch on her arrival in the Land of Oz.

Introduced under the simplified title *The Wizard of Oz*, the stage version opened in Chicago on June 16, 1902. From there it went to Broadway, where it opened the new Majestic Theater on Columbus Circle on January 21, 1903. New songs were written by A. Baldwin Sloane for the New York opening. It was a smash hit, and its run of 293 performances was phenomenal for that time. Its success brought Montgomery and Stone, who had been partners since 1895, Broadway stardom at last.

During the run, more songs were introduced. Two — *Sammy* and *Hurrah for Baffin's Bay* — became its biggest hits. *You're the Flower of My Heart, Sweet Adeline* was also worked in. Eventually, of the 17 songs used in the production, only three by Baum and Tietjens remained. They were *When You Love, Love, Love!* for Tinman, Dorothy and Scarecrow, *The Traveler and the Pie* for Scarecrow and chorus, and *Poppy Song* for chorus. More than anything, the play became a "musical extravaganza."

Its influence was considerable. The next production at the Majestic was the fairyland operetta *Babes in Toyland*, by

Fred Stone as the Scarecrow and David Montgomery as the Tin Woodman in the 1903 stage version of *The Wizard of Oz* [Courtesy of Performing Arts Research Center, The New York Public Library at Lincoln Center.]

43

The Wizard of Oz on stage in 1903: with the Scarecrow and others protesting, Dorothy is about to be beheaded by what could almost be a member of the Ku Klux Klan. Below right: a Baum–Tietjens number for the Tin Woodman, Dorothy and the Scarecrow published in the stage production's songbook. [Former: courtesy of Performing Arts Research Center, The New York Public Library at Lincoln Center.]

Victor Herbert and Glen McDonough. It unashamedly imitated *The Wizard of Oz* and presented living trees, an army of wood soldiers and other magical touches. Composer Herbert later wrote another comic operetta for Montgomery and Stone called *The Red Mill*.

Although *The Wizard of Oz* failed in a revival at the Majestic following *Babes in Toyland* in 1904, the musical toured with great success for the rest of the decade.

NEW OZ ADVENTURES

The Second Story of Oz

In 1904, Baum gave in to demands for another story of Oz. He was asked particularly for one about the Scarecrow and the Tin Woodman, for the stage musical had made them his best-known characters. In his Author's Note to the new book, *The Marvelous Land of Oz* (now known as *The Land of Oz*), he refers to letters imploring him to "write something more" about the two.

He relates how "Finally I promised one little girl, who made a long journey to see me and proffer her request — and she is a Dorothy, by the way — that when a thousand little girls had written me a thousand little letters asking for another story of the Scarecrow and the Tin Woodman, I would write the book. Either little Dorothy was a fairy in disguise, and waved her magic wand, or the success of the stage production of *The Wizard of Oz* made new friends for the story. For the thousand letters reached their destination long since — and many more followed them.

"And now, although pleading guilty to a long delay, I have kept my promise in this book."

His new story was set entirely in Oz and introduced some memorable characters. They included Jack Pumpkinhead, the Saw-Horse, the flying Gump and the Woggle-Bug, who shared adventures with the Scarecrow and Tin Woodman. Dorothy and the Cowardly Lion were not in the story this time. In fact, the Lion never played a major part in Baum's later Oz books.

The publishers, Reilly & Britton of Chicago, found a new illustrator to replace Denslow. He was John R. Neill, then only 26, also born in Philadelphia but younger than his predecessor and of more amiable temperament. Neill illustrated all the following Oz stories by Baum, as well as of those by Baum's successor. Neill eventually illustrated *and* wrote three Oz books on his own.

Baum hoped his second Oz book could be adapted for the stage with as much success as the earlier one. He called the play version of it *The Woggle-Bug*, to draw attention to its most conspicuous and amusing character. His book included a girl army that could be played by a line of chorus girls. He teamed the Woggle-Bug with Jack Pumpkinhead to make a new comic duo. The music for the show was written by Frederic Chapin, although the traditional nursery song *Patty Cake, Patty Cake, Baker's Man* was also included. It opened in Chicago on June 18, 1905, and lasted less than a month. Critics deemed it too childish and too simple. Baum and his colleagues evidently had not made the material appeal to mature audiences.

The flying Gump in action from *The Land of Oz* (1904). This contraption consists of two sofas strapped together, the head of a Gump, wings made of palm-leaves, and a broom for a tail. It is brought to life by the use of a magic powder.

Baum then turned to writing other children's books. *Queen Zixi of Ix, or the Story of the Magic Cloak* appeared in 1905. *John Dough and the Cherub* was published in 1906. More titles were produced under pseudonyms.

In 1906, Baum began the *Aunt Jane's Nieces* series for teenagers, using the name Edith van Dyne. The series contained 10 titles and the last was published in 1914. They enjoyed almost as much success as the Oz stories. In complete contrast with the Oz books, however, they dealt with the ugly problems of modern urban life as encountered by three nieces of a millionaire.

Baum also used the name Edith van Dyne for a series of *Mary Louise* books, writing five before his death. He wrote other stories for children as Floyd Akers (the *Boy Fortune Hunter* series, six books between 1908 and 1911), as Captain Hugh Fitzgerald (two *Sam Steele's Adventures*, 1906 and 1907), as Laura Bancroft and as Suzanne Metcalf. He also wrote two adult books as Schuyler Staunton. Another adult book, *The Last Egyptian*, was originally written anonymously in 1908 after a vacation in Egypt.

Baum used pseudonyms to avoid confusing the public, and to sell more books. He didn't want his real name too frequently on display in bookstores. It is important to remember he was always occupied on other books in addition to the Oz stories. But it was the Oz stories and other fairy tales that he wrote under his real name.

A Third Story – and a "Fairylogue"

In 1907 Baum responded to his young readers' pleas for "more about Dorothy" with the third Oz book, *Ozma of Oz*. The Cowardly Lion also reappeared accompanied by a new character, the Hungry Tiger. Billina, the talking yellow hen, made her debut. So did the clockwork man, Tik-Tok, the first manmade mechanical figure in literature (years before the word "robot" was invented).

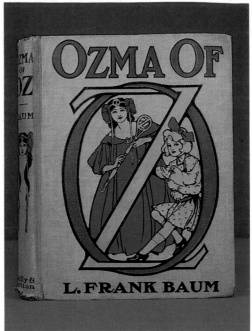

Most of the story occurs outside the Land of Oz, in the underground Nome kingdom. It concerns the efforts of Oz's ruler, Princess Ozma, to free the captive royal family of the nearby land of Ev.

With his interests in performing and showmanship, Baum hit on a novel idea to promote his three Oz books. In the early days of the movies, audiences were fascinated by travelogues (films of foreign places). He would give them "fairylogues" to show them the Land of Oz. He financed the project himself and called it *Fairylogue and Radio-Plays*. (The term "Radio-Plays" had nothing to do with broadcasting. It was a reference to the Frenchman Michel Radio, who had developed a technique for tinting film with transparent colors.)

The presentation involved Baum himself giving the introduction. He would then step out of sight and narrate over filmed scenes from the three published Oz books, another book (*John Dough and the Cherub*) and slides of illustrations from his next Oz book.

Made by the Selig Polyscope Co. in Chicago, the films had simple, but effective, trick effects. Two strips of films were combined to show the shipwrecked Dorothy in a stormy sea with Billina, from *Ozma of Oz*. A "lap dissolve" was used to show the boy Tip turning into the princess Ozma, from *The Land of Oz*. The flight of the Gump was assisted by invisible wires.

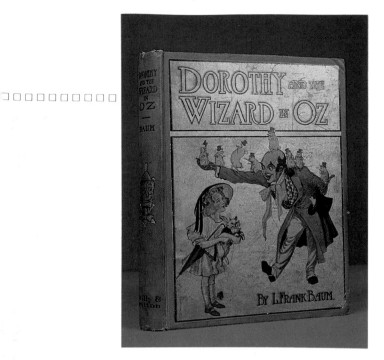

Dorothy (Romolo Remus) and friends as they appeared in *Fairylogue and Radio Plays* — the creature at front left is probably the Hungry Tiger, a companion of the Cowardly Lion. [Courtesy of Justin G. Schiller Ltd., New York.]

Far left: the cover of the fourth Oz adventure, published in 1908.

The show opened in Grand Rapids and Chicago to a warm reception. Unfortunately, Baum had not fully appreciated either the cost of making the films or of transporting the show, including musicians who provided a live accompaniment. Income failed to match expenditure, and Baum was forced to close the show in New York in December 1908.

Not everything was lost, though. Selig used the films to release four one-reelers in 1910. They were *The Wizard of Oz, Dorothy and Scarecrow in Oz, The Land of Oz* and *John Dough and the Cherub*. Some of the performers — Bebe Daniels, Hobart Bosworth and Eugenie Besserer, for example — are remembered for their later work in the movies.

More Excursions to Oz

The next Oz book, *Dorothy and the Wizard in Oz*, was published in 1908. In it, Baum's introductory remarks refer to "my loving tyrants," the children who demanded more stories of Oz. He states that he has replied to every letter he received, and that he has incorporated many of their suggestions.

I believe, my dears, that I am the proudest storyteller that ever lived. Many a time tears of pride and joy have stood in my eyes while I read the tender, loving, appealing letters that come to me in almost every mail from my little readers. To have pleased you, to have interested you, to have won your friendship, and perhaps your love, through my stories, is to my mind as great an achievement as to become President of the United States.

It was in this volume that by popular demand he brought back the Wizard. This book also introduced readers to Jim the Cab-Horse, the Nine Tiny Piglets and Eureka the kitten who wants to eat them.

A fifth Oz book, *The Road to Oz* (1909), returned Toto to Oz, again in response to readers' demands. Baum also introduced them to the Shaggy Man, Polychrome the Rainbow's daughter, and the dim-witted Button-Bright. In the preface, Baum declared that he had now received "some very remarkable news" from Oz which he was saving for his next book. He warned that "perhaps that book will be the last story that will ever be told about the Land of Oz."

The final chapter of *The Emerald City of Oz* (1910) made his plan clear. In his introduction he described himself as "merely an editor or private secretary for a host of youngsters whose ideas I am requested to weave into the thread of my stories." He revealed that Dorothy and her Aunt Em and Uncle Henry were permanently settled in Oz in compliance with his readers' wishes. This made it possible for Dorothy to live there happily ever after. The story deals with the Nome King's strenuous efforts to conquer Oz and Princess Ozma's decision to safeguard the country by making it invisible. Baum concludes the book with a coda that reads like a stop-press item. He reports receiving a farewell letter from Dorothy in which she says:

You will never hear anything more about Oz, because we are now cut off forever from all the rest of the world. But Toto and I will always love you and all the other children who love us.

Mr. Baum Goes to Hollywood

For some years, L. Frank Baum and his wife escaped Chicago winter by traveling. In 1907, they went to Egypt and Europe. For the next three years they lived in Coronado, California, where Baum completed the Oz books published in 1908, 1909 and 1910. Deciding to settle in California, the couple looked for a place near a big city to provide employment for the boys after they finished school. The small town with orange trees that they chose was Hollywood. Using money Maud inherited in 1910, they bought a plot of land a block from Hollywood Boulevard. There they built a frame house that they called Ozcot.

Having publicly said farewell to Oz, Baum wrote two different children's fantasies, *The Sea Fairies* (1911) and *Sky Island* (1912). (The latter included two Oz characters, Button-Bright and Poly-chrome.) The books were illustrated by John R. Neill, but they did not sell as well as the Oz books. After Baum slid into bankruptcy in June 1911, he had no choice but to call once more upon the magic of Oz in an attempt to restore his fortunes.

Baum tried first for another stage success. He wrote *The Tik-Tok Man of Oz* for a Los Angeles impresario, working with composer Louis F. Gottschalk. Opening with a spectacular storm-at-sea sequence, the production featured a new girl heroine, Betsy Bobbin, and another pantomime animal, Hank the Mule. Hank was played by an expert at such impersonations, Fred Woodward.

Humor resided in the relationship between Tik-Tok, a metallic figure in the tradition of the Tin Woodman, and the Shaggy Man with his love-inducing magnet, who looked like a Scarecrow. The two were played by the comedy team of James C. Morton and Frank Y. Moore. Polychrome also appeared in the story. Charlie Ruggles, later a leading character actor in Hollywood, was featured as Private Files of

the Oogaboo Army of Queen Ann Soforth, who was played by Charlotte Greenwood, also well-known for subsequent movie work.

With these elements, plus a chorus line of leggy beauties to portray the Rose Kingdom, and with such eye-catching sets as the underground domain of the Nome King Ruggedo, the production was skilfully devised on the lines of the stage *Wizard of Oz*. For one reviewer, it "conjured up the days when extravaganzas dominated the American stage." The same critic, punning on Tik-Tok's clockwork mechanism, thought the play was "wound up for a long run." It did do well, although it never reached New York.

At Ozcot, Baum finished a new Oz book, *The Patchwork Girl of Oz* (1913). In the prologue, he described himself as the Royal Historian of Oz, and mentioned the

demand for stories of Oz before it severed connections with the rest of the world. Finally, he declared "One of the children inquired why we couldn't hear from Princess Dorothy by wireless telegraph." This became Baum's device for re-establishing contact. He pretended he had obtained a new story by telegraph directly from Dorothy, with the gracious consent of Ozma. The seventh in the series, the book described the quest of Ojo, a Munchkin boy, to find the magical cure to restore his uncle to life after he has accidentally been turned to stone. It also introduced Scraps, the Patchwork Girl.

The Oz Film Manufacturing Company

Baum could hardly help noticing that the film industry was booming around him. Selig had built a studio at Edendale in August 1909, although the first studio in Hollywood did not open for production until October 1911. Cecil B. DeMille was not the first Hollywood film-maker when he arrived to shoot *The Squaw Man* at the end of 1913. It was just at this time the idea arose of organizing a company to make Oz films.

The Shaggy Man's expertise with the telegraph helps restore communications with the Land of Oz — a John R. Neill illustration from *The Patchwork Girl of Oz* (1913). [Courtesy of Contemporary Books Inc., Chicago.]

Baum was a founding member of a social club that included businessmen, performers and other creative figures from the screen and theater worlds. Called The Uplifters, it met each Saturday at noon at the Los Angeles Athletic Club. It was there that the Oz Film Manufacturing Co. came into being. L. Frank Baum contributed the rights to those books he still owned (some had been yielded to his creditors) and was made president. Louis F. Gottschalk agreed to write the scores for the live musicians to accompany the silent films, and he was elected vice-president. Other club members became treasurer and secretary, and quickly raised the capital.

A 7-acre site was acquired at Colegrove in South Hollywood, between Gower and Lodi Streets on Santa Monica Boulevard. A studio and laboratories were built, and Baum devised a large, enclosed stage. Underneath the floor, he included a concrete-lined tunnel and several tanks that could be used to create indoor rivers and lakes. The tunnels and tanks also enabled actors to disappear from sight through trapdoors.

In 1914, the Oz Film Manufacturing Co. made sure the movie business knew of its impending arrival. An advertising campaign threw modesty to the winds. Baum's picture was circulated with a declaration that his "genius makes possible a newer and better era in Motion Pictures." The company letterhead proclaimed it to be a producer of "Special Features in Fairy Extravaganzas with Original Music." And a program was announced of monthly releases running 30 minutes to an hour.

Production began in the summer. The first film was *The Patchwork Girl of Oz*, a version of Baum's latest book. It was previewed at the Club on August 6, 1914, and was of course "silent", like all movies of this period. The company then made *The Magic Cloak of Oz*, an adaptation of Baum's 1905 book *Queen Zixi of Ix* that had nothing to do with the Land of Oz. After that came *His Majesty, the Scarecrow of Oz*, a new story with many familiar

The film company letterhead. [Courtesy of the International Wizard of Oz Club.]

characters, including Dorothy and the Tin Woodman.

Paramount released *The Patchwork Girl of Oz* in September 1914 to tepid response. According to Baum's oldest son, writing in *Films in Review* in 1956, "Patrons complained about theaters showing 'kid stories' and some even demanded their money back." Not one distributor would handle *The Magic Cloak of Oz*. A minor company took *His Majesty, The Scarecrow of Oz* only after it had been agreed to retitle it *The New Wizard of Oz*, in the hope of cashing in on earlier success.

All three films survive and are dealt with in more detail later.

In desperation, the Oz company changed course. By December 1914, a modern drama, *The Last Egyptian*, was ready for release. Originally Baum had written the source novel anonymously, but now his name appeared as author. The highlights of the film were the exotic settings, an action-packed fight-to-the-death in a treasure tomb and "The Famous Oz Cast of Beautiful Women." It is a story of racial conflict, and may surprise many readers of the Oz tales.

It concerns the revenge exacted on an English earl by a handsome young Egyptian, Kara, for the betrayal of his grandmother. Kara puts the earl's family in debt to him by beating the aristocrat's son at cards. His sister, the daughter of the family, agrees to marry Kara in order to save the family from disgrace. A young explorer, who loves the girl, persuades her to run away with him, but Kara enlists the aid of bandits to capture them. To pay their leader, Kara visits a secret tomb for money. At the tomb, however, he is surprised and captured by the earl, who locks him away to die. The earl is then himself killed by an embittered Egyptian girl who mistakes him for Kara. The unpaid

bandits withdraw, freeing the daughter and the young explorer.

The film still used the Oz name and had many of the same players as earlier films. Exhibitors were too suspicious to book it widely, and the company's crisis was unresolved.

The Later Books of Baum

Baum produced two books in 1914 — *Aunt Jane's Nieces Out West* (under the nom-de-plume Edith van Dyne) and *Tik-Tok of Oz*. The latter was based on the stage play, *The Tik-Tok Man of Oz*, which was no longer running. Baum was still careful to insert an introductory note advising his readers the book contained fresh material, lest they be deterred from buying it.

He also said that children had been urging him to introduce Trot and Cap'n Bill — the little Californian girl and the old one-legged sea salt of his non-Oz books, *The Sea Fairies* and *Sky Island* — into the realm of Oz. He teased readers with the news that this had happened and that all would be explained in his next book.

This paved the way for *The Scarecrow of Oz* (1915). The book began with the various adventures of Trot and Cap'n Bill before arriving in Oz. It then lapsed into the story from the film *His Majesty, The Scarecrow of Oz*, in which Trot replaced Dorothy.

Also in 1915, at the beginning of April, the Oz film company reopened the studios to make a topical war drama. Entitled *The Gray Nun of Belgium*, it was about a nun who helped Allied soldiers trapped behind enemy lines to return to their own side. However, no distributor wanted it, and the film was never released. The studio was subsequently leased to outside producers for a few months, then the company was disbanded. Baum recovered the movie rights he had contributed to the company.

In 1916, the eager reading public was presented with *Rinkitink in Oz*. It was very largely a reworking of a fantasy story Baum had written more than 10 years earlier. Only the conclusion took place in Oz,

John R. Neill depicts the Tin Woodman's encounter with another tin figure in *The Tin Woodman of Oz* (1918). [Courtesy of Contemporary Books Inc., Chicago.]

Cover of the 1920 Oz book, the last by L. Frank Baum, showing Glinda in different headgear from that in earlier Neill drawings (such as the one on page 20). [Courtesy of Contemporary Books Inc., Chicago.]

although the familiar underground world of the Nomes was featured in the plot.

If Baum was running out of ideas for Oz stories, he had only to listen to his readers. In the preface to his 1917 book, *The Lost Princess of Oz*, he wrote "I must admit that the main idea . . . was suggested to me by a sweet little girl of 11 who called to see me and to talk about the Land of Oz. Said she: 'I s'pose if Ozma ever got lost, or stolen, ev'rybody in Oz would be dreadful sorry.'" This spurred Baum to write one of his most imaginative tales.

The following year, the Royal Historian of Oz in the introduction to his next volume, *The Tin Woodman of Oz*, promised it would please certain readers in particular. They were the many correspondents who had wanted to know what became of the Munchkin girl that the Tin Woodman had been engaged to marry before he axed himself to pieces. By this time, the books had become established as an annual treat, and Baum concluded by promising some astonishing revelations about the magic of Oz in his book for 1919.

The Tin Woodman of Oz itself had had some amazing discoveries in its later chapters. The Tin Woodman encounters another tin figure, finds his own head still living in a cupboard and discovers another figure partially constructed of his discarded parts! Baum had virtually taken Oz readers into Frankenstein's laboratory!

He also quoted letters from readers aged 5 to 70 years old. "My books are intended for all those whose hearts are young, no matter what their ages may be." But Baum's own heart was not as young as it had been. As a child, it was thought he had a defective heart. In 1917, his gall bladder began to give trouble, and he reluctantly entered a hospital to have it removed. He never properly recovered from the strain on his heart, and he spent the rest of his life largely confined to bed in his Hollywood home.

In his 1919 book, *The Magic of Oz*, the author's prefatory remarks referred to his health. "A long and confining illness has prevented my answering all the good letters sent me — unless stamps were enclosed — but from now on I hope to be able to give prompt attention to each and every letter with which my readers favor me." Fortunately, his condition did not prevent him from constructing another story. It combined another of the Nome King Ruggedo's attempts to conquer Oz with familiar Oz characters gathering presents for Ozma's birthday party.

But his 14th book, *Glinda of Oz*, was published posthumously in 1920. In it, Ozma made a rare trip out of the Emerald City to prevent strife between the Skeezers and Flatheads, two groups in the outer reaches of Gillikin country.

The publishers provided the foreword and introduced the story. To it they added a notice.

Mr. Baum did his best to answer all the letters from his small earth-friends before he had to leave them, but he couldn't answer quite all, for there were very many. In May, nineteen hundred nineteen, he went away to take his stories to the little child-souls who had lived here too long ago to read the Oz stories for themselves.

Their cloying words missed the unpatronizing tone Baum had so successfully managed in his introductions. The publishers added that Baum had left some notes about Dorothy, Princess Ozma and the people of Oz. They were hoping to assemble something from the notes for future publication.

When the Royal Historian of Oz died on May 6, 1919, he was the most celebrated children's author of his time. His last words were said to be "Now we can cross the Shifting Sands . . ." The Shifting Sands are the barrier that prevents mortals from entering the Land of Oz via Munchkin Country. The Royal Historian was going home.

THE APPEAL OF OZ

Little Girls' Delight

The splendor of Ozma Royal Palace of Oz dominates this Neill illustration from *The Road to Oz* (1909). The Wizard greets the Scarecrow and the Tin Woodman while Jack Pumpkinhead looks on from the landing.

If Baum's books were aimed at children, their appeal was especially to little girls. From Dorothy Gale to Ozma, the wise and benificent Ruler of Oz, almost all his strong figures are female. His trio of the Scarecrow, the Tin Woodman and the Cowardly Lion have real and imagined deficiencies. The Scarecrow is easily toppled from the throne when he attempts to rule Oz in the Wizard's place in *The Land of Oz*.

Button-Bright is a very slow-witted, helpless boy who knows nothing and is always wandering off and becoming lost. Tip, in *The Land of Oz*, is brave and resourceful despite being "small and rather delicate in appearance". But he turns out to be really a girl — Ozma, the rightful ruler of Oz.

Even when wrong, female characters are strong-willed and decisive. The beautiful vegetable princess of the Mangaboos in *Dorothy and the Wizard in Oz* ungratefully rejects the visitors who brought her to life. Jinjur, in *The Land of Oz*, musters an army of girls, appoints herself General, arms her troops with knitting needles, and finally conquers the Emerald City. It takes another army of girls under Glinda the Good Witch to mount an effective counterattack.

Baum's years at military academy seem to have left him with a scathing contempt for officers. There is a valiant private in the Army of Oz, but its eight generals, six colonels, seven majors and five captains in *Ozma of Oz* are all cowards. In *Tik-Tok of Oz*, a colonel of a different army (the Army of Ogaboo) declares, "I myself am brave as a lion in all ways until it comes to fighting, and then my nature revolts. Fighting is unkind and liable to be injurious to others; so, being a gentleman, I never fight."

Only in his last book, *Glinda of Oz*, does Baum introduce an intelligent, resourceful young man, Ervic, who helps save his people, the Skeezers. But he does not fill the vacancy for a new local ruler. He has to settle for being prime minister under a new Queen, Lady Aurex.

Baum depicts a world in which women rule and have power. In magic and sorcery, the main practitioners are all women. The Wizard of Oz, conversely, is an admitted humbug who is only later taught real magic by Glinda.

Dr. Pipt is a male magician in *The Patchwork Girl of Oz*, and his Powder of Life is miraculously effective. But it takes him nearly 6 years of stirring four kettles over a fire to make the compound. Others, like Ugu the Shoemaker (*The Lost Princess of Oz*) and the Nome King (various books), have some magical powers but these are shortlived. The giantess Mrs. Yoop (*The Tin Woodman of Oz*), on the other hand, is far more cunning and resourceful.

Girl readers can find many figures with whom to identify, and Oz is described in terms most likely to appeal to them. There is an emphasis on jewelry, fine costumes and dressing up. Everything is "beautiful," "gorgeous" or "lovely" in Ozma's palace.

Dorothy had four lovely rooms in the palace, which were always reserved for her use and were called 'Dorothy's rooms.' These consisted of a beautiful sitting room, a dressing room, a

Authority in Oz

dainty bedchamber and a big marble bathroom. And in these rooms were everything the heart could desire, placed there with loving thoughtfulness by Ozma for her little friend's use. The royal dressmakers had the little girl's measure, so they kept the closets in her dressing room filled with lovely dresses of every description and suitable for every occasion. No wonder Dorothy had refrained from bringing with her old calico and gingham dresses! Here everything that was dear to a little girl's heart was supplied in profusion, and nothing so rich and beautiful could ever have been found in the biggest department stores in America.

The Emerald City abounds in precious gems. Its gates are jewel-encrusted. The sidewalks are slabs of marble, the curbs set with emeralds. Its buildings are covered in gold plate and emeralds. Even the golden handcuffs are studded with rubies and diamonds. Glinda's palace is just as lavishly appointed, down to the jewels on the padlocks to her Book of Records.

The statement by Betsy Bobbin, a normal American girl, after she has sampled the pleasures of life in the Emerald City in *Tik-Tok of Oz*, comes as no surprise. "I didn't believe any girl could ever have such a good time — *anywhere* — as I'm having now." She remarks, "I wish that every little girl in the world could live in the Land of Oz; and every little boy, too!" (Little boys seem brought in as an afterthought!)

Even Dorothy comes to prefer Oz to Kansas. "There's no place like home" — but home means Aunt Em and Uncle Henry. After she has arranged for them all to live in Oz, there is no reason to go back. In particular, she is a Princess in Oz, but "when I'm back home in Kansas I'm only a country girl, and have to help with the churning and wipe the dishes while Aunt Em washes 'em." What initially is a fantasy for Dorothy becomes reality when she settles permanently in the Land of Oz.

Part of the appeal of the Oz stories was the figures of royalty created in the European tradition. This meant that there could be pomp and ceremony, Kings and Queens, Emperors and Empresses, Ladies and Princesses. Yet official authority is used only for the benefit of all. It is said of Ozma (in *The Scarecrow of Oz*) that "Her happy subjects adore their girl Ruler and each one considers her a comrade and protector." (It is unfortunate that since those days the terms "comrade" and "protector" have come to have authoritarian overtones.)

At the same time, Baum cannot resist puncturing the wonderful aura he ascribes to those in positions of power. He tells us in a footnote in *Ozma of Oz* that even a princess has to do common things like darn stockings. In *The Tin Woodman of Oz* he presents the Loons, who have deliberately chosen the most stupid of their members to be King, knowing leadership involves hard work and responsibility. Baum's work is enriched by this complexity of attitude. It is never one-dimensional.

Oz has an absolute ruler, but she never takes advantage of her position. The fairyland is a place of equality where no one has money or wealth, and it is an example to other countries. As the Tin Woodman says, in *The Road to Oz*,

If we used money to buy things with, instead of love and kindness and the desire to please one another, then we should be no better than the rest of the world. Fortunately money is not known in the Land of Oz at all. We have no rich, and no poor; for what one wishes the others all try to give him, in order to make him happy, and no one in Oz cares to have more than he can use.

In the civilized parts of Oz, there is almost no crime, so there is no need for a police force. The most common offense, or suspected offense, is eating animals. (Eureka the Kitten stands trial for eating a

Ozma looks at her Magic Picture with Dorothy standing behind (and another girl visitor to Oz, Betsy Bobbin, in the background). From *The Scarecrow of Oz* (1915).
[Courtesy of Contemporary Books Inc., Chicago.]

Horrific image: the Wizard slices the Sorcerer in half — John R. Neill's vivid illustration from *Dorothy and the Wizard in Oz* (1908).

piglet in *Dorothy and the Wizard in Oz*.) In Oz, all animals are treated with as much respect as people, as long as they behave. "Flies like to be treated politely as well as other creatures, and here in Oz they understand what we say to them, and behave very nicely," explains the Wizard in *The Emerald City of Oz*.

Even when Oz is threatened by evil hordes in the same book, Ozma refuses to fight. She explains that "No one has the right to destroy any living creature, however evil they may be, or to hurt them or make them unhappy. I will not fight — even to save my kingdom." In any case, by conventional standards, Ozma has no defense. As the Wizard points out, "The present army is composed only of officers, and the business of an officer is to order his men to fight. Since there are no men there can be no fighting."

Baum's views, as expressed in the Oz books, leaned toward a society that is non-competitive and essentially altruistic. He favors one in which people enjoy their work and in which pacifism is the official policy. If Baum's books had not been kept off library shelves until the 1960s for their alleged lack of literary merit, they might have been banned as politically subversive for the ideas they gave the young.

Yet, oddly enough, Baum's Oz has something in common with George Orwell's *1984*. Just as Big Brother can look into every home via the telescreen, Ozma has her Magic Picture. "If I wish to see any part of the world or any person living, I need only express the wish, and it is shown in the picture" (*Ozma of Oz*). Of course Ozma uses it only for the best of reasons, and it helps to rescue Dorothy and friends from a tight spot in *Dorothy and the Wizard in Oz*. But it could fall into the wrong hands — and does, when Ugu the Shoemaker steals it in *The Lost Princess of Oz*.

Enigmas of Oz

Baum's 14 books vary in quality, even within individual volumes. To some extent, this is because he did not set out with a grand plan for a series (as did George Lucas with the film *Star Wars*). Only in response to market pressure did he write the second Oz book. Then, when he realized he had erred in omitting Dorothy from it, he wrote a third book that included her — but not until 7 years after *The Wizard of Oz* had appeared. An attempt to end the series was made with the sixth title in 1910. But from 1913 on, Baum provided other Oz books at yearly intervals until his death. At the same time he was also busy writing other books under various pseudonyms.

So it is not surprising that inconsistencies crept in. Where characterization is concerned, the most notable example is that of the Wizard. In the second book, *The Land of Oz*, he is a wicked figure who practices real magic and usurps the throne of the Emerald City. He arranges that the baby heir, Ozma, should be kept hidden away. In later books, however, he reverts to being the admitted humbug of the original work and is a man who is loved and trusted. Slowly, he learns real magic from Glinda. In Baum's last Oz book, *Glinda of Oz*, he even becomes a clear-thinking, decisive figure.

In *The Wizard of Oz*, the Emerald City isn't really green. It only looks green because of the tinted spectacles that anyone who lives or visits there must wear. In time, this cumbersome device is dropped.

Geographically, there are other variations. Munchkin country was originally established as being in the east part of Oz, and Winkie country in the west. But the map that appeared as the end-papers in *Tik-Tok of Oz* in 1914 shows them reversed. (The map was attributed to Professor Woggle-Bug, so perhaps the blame attaches to that eminent pedant!)

Glinda is usually the Good Witch of the South, and her castle or palace is located to the south of Oz. But in *Tik-Tok of Oz* the palace is situated (by unremarked magic?) in the north. (And to complicate matters, the 1939 film also had Glinda coming from the north.)

These and many other problems have vexed the scholars of Oz and produced ingenious explanations. For some, there is simply no convincing solution. Baum wrote himself into corners he would have avoided had he known he would be touching upon the same ground later. When he stated that no money was used in Oz, he probably hoped readers would not recall the ferryman asking for money in his second book. When he had the Shaggy Man declare that his love-inducing magnet worked in Butterfield, *outside* fairyland, he was being a little careless.

But it is silly to dwell on small details in the face of Baum's obvious overall success in appealing to his readers. An interesting essay for *The Baum Bugle*, the magazine of the International Wizard of Oz Club, focused on this subject. In "Oz and the Fifth Criterion," C. Warren Hollister was prepared to concede that the 14 Oz books by Baum were deficient in theme, characterization, plot and style, compared with the work of other famous writers of children's books. He rightly insisted, however, that the books deserved critical attention because of their indisputable appeal. He attributed this to another, unrecognized factor in which the books excelled — their "three-dimensionality."

"It is the magical tugging of the

Dorothy and the Wizard reassemble the Cook who has fallen to bits in Fuddlecumjig. A Neill illustration from *The Emerald City of Oz* (1910).

"I'M THE COOK".

child-reader through the page into the story — into the other world," declared Hollister. "You not only suspend disbelief in Oz; you not only positively, ardently believe in Oz; you are there!"

Of course, it was not just the text. It was also the skill of the illustrators that achieved this effect. Certainly Oz was real enough for one major writer, John Steinbeck. His greatest wish, he once said, was to be the United States' Ambassador to Oz.

Part of Baum's technique was to break down the barrier between himself and his young readers. He sometimes talked to them directly. In *The Magic of Oz*, Baum revealed a word that caused magical transformations if uttered. ". . . I would not dare to write down this magic word so plainly if I thought my readers would pronounce it properly and so be able to transform themselves and others, but it is fact that no one in all the world except Bini Aru, had ever (up to the time this book begins) been able to pronounce 'P y r z q x g l !' the right way, so I think it is safe to give it to you."

In fact, Baum had such a grasp on his readers that he dared to remind them that he had created the stories. This happened in *Tik-Tok of Oz*. Betsy Bobbin and the Shaggy Man are searching for the underground cavern of Ruggedo, the Metal Monarch (Nome King):

"We may find it ourselves, without any help," suggested Betsy. "Who knows?"

"No one knows that, except the person who's writing this story," said Shaggy.

Endless Inventiveness

Baum was not a great master of story construction. He delighted more in characters and settings. It was of no consequence to him how much coincidence, contrivance or damage to pace was caused by his bright ideas. He liked to think of a substance and devise a people or country made from it. The china people of *The Wizard of Oz* were the first of many.

In isolation, such character-creations can be amusing. But in *The Emerald City of Oz*, Baum clogs the narrative with seven of them. These are the Cuttenclips (living cut-out paper dolls), the Fuddles of Fuddlecumjig (people who break apart and must be reassembled like jigsaw puzzles), the living kitchen utensils of Utensia, and the Flutterbudgets (people who worry needlessly about everything). In addition, he created Bunbury (where people are made of buns or bread, move on sidewalks of breadcrusts and live in houses made of crackers), Bunnybury (where rabbits live in luxury in a city of marble) and Rigmarole Town (whose inhabitants talk without ever getting to the point).

In his 1954 study of *Who's Who in Oz*, Jack Snow lists 220 entries for Baum characters. Many characters are unnecessary duplications. His American girls — Dorothy, Betsy Bobbin and Trot — are not very different from each other. The Frogman is really a reworking of the Woggle-Bug. Instead of developing old characters, he preferred to devise new variations.

Similarly, Baum was not content with exploring Oz and its distinctive regions. He also introduced neighboring fantasy countries. It is in these that most of *Dorothy and the Wizard in Oz* and *Rinkitink in Oz* takes place. They reflect a remarkable capacity for invention, but they also make the stories unnecessarily complicated.

Baum sometimes resorts to the magic of Oz to conjure up instant solutions to tight spots. In *Dorothy and the Wizard in Oz*, Dorothy and her companions escape from many dangers through their own initiative, only to end up in a dark cavern underground with nowhere to go. At this point, Baum tells us Ozma always looks for Dorothy in her Magic Picture at four o' clock every afternoon. Dorothy has only to give a prearranged sign to be whisked off to Oz. She escapes there and brings the others immediately afterward — end of problem.

In *The Emerald City of Oz*, the Nome General Guph makes a tremendous effort to recruit other evil-minded nations and launches a secret invasion of the Emerald City by tunnel. It is disappointing to learn Ozma has known all about it through her Magic Picture and won't be taken by surprise.

In *The Patchwork Girl of Oz*, Dorothy and her friends spend most of the book collecting the various items needed to provide an antidote for petrifaction. (Other characters have been accidentally turned to stone.) Glinda, however, simply instructs the Wizard on how to destroy the spell, and provides another anticlimax.

put the spout to the mouth of the girl and gave her a big drink "

Although Baum did not make his later books as gruesome as the first, he still provided a fair number of violent and disturbing incidents. In the second book, the Tin Woodman wields his ax against jackdaws just as he had fought wolves in the first book. But this time there is no mention of any being killed.

In fact, the most horrifying moment in the Oz canon occurs in the fourth book, *Dorothy and the Wizard in Oz*. To overcome a spell that had stopped his breathing, the Wizard raised a sharp sword and "whirled it once or twice around his head, and then gave a mighty stroke that cut the body of the Sorcerer exactly in two. Dorothy screamed . . ." As must many of Baum's more sensitive readers! The slicing of the Sorcerer is also vividly illustrated by Neill. But Baum shows his ingenuity as a storyteller. "As the two halves of the Sorcerer fell apart on the floor, [Dorothy] saw that he had no bones or blood inside of him at all, and that the place where he was cut looked much like a sliced turnip or potato." Only now is he revealed as a vegetable person!

For *The Patchwork Girl of Oz*, Baum originally devised other vegetable people. They cultivate plants that grow human heads, which are presumably picked and eaten. Here the publishers felt Baum had gone too far. Baum agreed to take the episode out. It was a self-contained chapter and so could be deleted without upsetting the surrounding text. The author did not abandon the concept, however. In his next book, rulers of the Rose Kingdom grow on royal bushes in the royal gardens and are picked when fully grown, then come to life. At least they were not regarded as food or placed in any danger.

In the books, there are many alarming moments. The Scarecrow often loses his straw, and Jack Pumpkinhead loses his head. But they are easily restored. Less fortunate are the unfriendly Scoodlers of *The Road to Oz*, who use their heads as missiles. The Shaggy Man fails to throw them back and instead consigns them to a deep pit.

These are the dark sides to Baum's vision that contrast with the lighter aspects. Life in and around Oz is always unpredictable!

Baum's sense of humor, though not widely admired, is resourceful and imaginative. He relied heavily on puns. The Woggle-Bug even defends the pun in *The Land of Oz*. " . . . I say that puns display genius. For instance, were I to ride upon this Saw-Horse, he would not only be an animal — he would become an equipage. For he would then be a horse-and-buggy."

In *The Patchwork Girl of Oz*, there are people called Horners who incessantly tell bad jokes. Their joke (that their one-legged neighbors the Hoppers must have less *under-standing* than Horners with two legs) results in a high fence, like an Iron Curtain, separating the two groups.

Dorothy on trial in Utensia, from *The Emerald City of Oz* (1910).

The books' tongue-in-cheek ideas on education must have produced a warmly appreciative response from many readers. Professor Woggle-Bug, the Principal of the Royal Athletic College, provides his scholars with tablets to eat after breakfast. These give knowledge of different subjects, including math, good handwriting and spelling. "It mattered not whether a boy or girl was stupid or bright, for the tablets taught them everything in the twinkling of an eye," we are told in *The Land of Oz*. This "allows the students to devote all their time to racing, baseball, tennis and other manly and womanly sports."

Baum's keen grasp of the ridiculous keeps many of his ideas from being merely silly. At times they are surreal, as when characters paint pictures that look so natural they become real. The co-inventor of Tik-Tok drowns in a painted river (*Ozma of Oz*), and the Scarecrow refills his body from a painted stack of straw (*The Tin Woodman of Oz*).

It is the same with verbal humor. A sequence worthy of a Groucho and Chico Marx duologue occurs in *The Land of Oz*.

His Majesty the Scarecrow meets Jack Pumpkinhead for the first time. An interpreter is summoned, even though only one language is spoken in Oz. "Won't you take a chair while we are waiting?" asks the Scarecrow. "Your Majesty forgets that I cannot understand you," replies Jack . . .

At Dorothy's trial in Utensia (*The Emerald City of Oz*), various living kitchen implements swap outrageous puns and Dorothy (like Alice in *Alice in Wonderland* in similar circumstances) is cool and collected even though she is on trial for her life. This is another example of a sustained sketch that reads like a vaudeville piece.

Perhaps the most intricate visual imagery occurs in *The Lost Princess of Oz*. Dorothy, the Wizard and others see a magic image of what Ugu the Shoemaker is viewing in the Magic Picture that he stole from Ozma. They see themselves as Ugu sees them, from behind. The image of the group watching the image is repeated, smaller and smaller, ad infinitum . . .

Who's looking at who? Dorothy and friends see themselves as their opponent Ugu the Shoemaker sees them in the stolen Magic Picture. From *The Lost Princess of Oz* (1917). [Courtesy of Contemporary Books Inc., Chicago.]

Baum's Oz Films Revisited

Pierre Couderc in the title role of the 1914 Oz silent film, *The Patchwork Girl of Oz.*

ivian Reed's smile reeted the audience at ne start of the Oz film ompany's features. She vas based on Ozma as rawn by John R. Neill.

The Oz Film Manufacturing Company had a charming trademark. Its films opened with the smiling features of Vivian Reed, dressed as Ozma. She wore a band with the name Oz across her forehead and turned her face from side to side. (This image anticipates the smiling lady who bowed at the start of Britain's Gainsborough Pictures.)

The Patchwork Girl of Oz cast a woman (Violet MacMillan) as Ojo, the Munchkin boy, following the pantomime tradition. Frank Moore and Fred Woodward were recruited from the cast of the stage play *The Tik-Tok Man of Oz.* Moore played Ojo's uncle, who is inadvertently turned to stone. Woodward filled out the costumes of the four-legged figures, like the square-shaped Woozy and the Mule.

The title character, Scraps, the Patchwork Girl, was portrayed by Pierre Couderc — "The Marvelous Couderc (Positively first American appearance, on Stage or Screen)." He was a lanky French acrobat who gave a suitably exuberant interpretation of the figure brought to life by magic powder.

The movie was a simplified adaptation of the most recent book of that time, but it also made changes. The Glass Cat and the Living Phonograph, other results of the magic powder, were omitted because of difficulties in presenting them. Romantic interest was added between two Munchkin figures, Jesseva and Danx, and complicated when Danx is turned into a stone statue and shrunk to pocketsize. In that form he is coveted by the girl Jinjur, who is in charge of an army of beautiful girls at the Emerald City. Dorothy and the Cowardly Lion are not seen, but the Scarecrow is prominent; he falls in love with the Patchwork Girl. The Tin Woodman and Wizard of Oz also appear briefly at the end.

Frame enlargement of the actual opening title of Baum's own 1914 film about Oz.

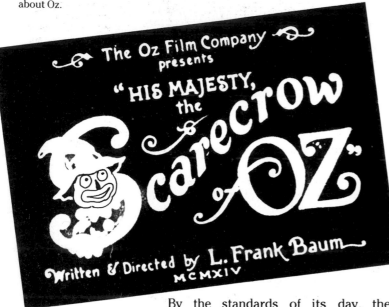

By the standards of its day, the production was somewhat primitive. (A trade review criticized its acting and photography.) It certainly introduced an array of characters that would have confused anyone unfamiliar with the Oz books. The natural outdoor locations tended to overwhelm the fantasy. Such fantastic figures looked absurd without correspondingly fantastic settings.

Some movie magic was used in the picture, such as stop-action photography and superimposition. Special effects included the lightning assembly of the pieces that make up the Patchwork Girl on a table before she is dusted with the powder of life. Characters walk through an illusory wall. A table is laid and a piping hot meal is set down by unseen hands. The miniature Danx is restored to life and enlarged to his normal size by the Wizard.

The film contains a touch of Baum humor not found in the book. One character visits the one-legged Hoppers, who want to cut off one of his legs. Finally, they settle instead for a leg belonging to the Patchwork Girl, which of course can be restored later.

Certainly the reviewer recognized *The Patchwork Girl of Oz* was "children's entertainment". He added, though, he would be "quick to recommend it to every exhibitor." Most newspaper reviews were complimentary, and its failure at the box office came as a surprise.

The next film, *The Magic Cloak of Oz* had almost no connection with Oz. The Fairies of Oz put a magic cloak in the country of Noland at the start — and that is the only way Oz is mentioned. But the movie was clearly aimed at children. It centers on a boy king, Bud, who spends his entire treasury buying the contents of a toyshop. (Bud, and Queen Zixi of neighboring Ix, turned up as guests at Princess Ozma's birthday party in the Oz book, *The Road to Oz*.)

The most memorable figures are a variation on the soup-loving Scoodlers of *The Road to Oz*. In this movie they become the Rolly Rogues who (according to a title) run round the ragged rocks. These round, brainless creatures conquer Noland to force the inhabitants to make them a new kind of soup.

These two films were directed by J. Farrell MacDonald (still remembered today as a supporting actor in John Ford and Preston Sturges movies). L. Frank Baum not only wrote but directed the third film, *His Majesty, the Scarecrow of Oz*.

For this film he revived a couple of his notions from *The Wizard of Oz*. Dorothy finds the Tin Woodman rusted stiff again and oils his joints. And the Scarecrow tries to steer a raft and is left dangling from a pole, to be carried to the riverbank by a large crow (a stork in the book).

In this story, the blond Dorothy (again Violet MacMillan) is a slave or servant of the witch Mombi (Mai Wells). She watches the witch freeze the heart of Princess Gloria (Vivian Reed) on instructions from wicked King Krewl in order to stop her loving Pon, a mere gardener's boy. The Tin

This series of frame enlargements from *His Majesty, the Scarecrow of Oz* shows the witch Mombi (Mai Wells, with eye-patch) receiving orders to freeze the heart of Princess Gloria (Vivian Reed, bound to a post) and, with the help of a chorus of younger witches and some elementary special effects, extracting the heart and changing its appearance. [Courtesy of Em Gee Film Library.]

The Tin Castle of the Tin Woodman.

Woodman (Pierre Couderc) organizes a group to capture King Krewl and force him to restore Gloria's heart. The Scarecrow (Frank Moore) leads the attack on the King's castle because the barrage of arrows have no effect on him. They are victorious and the Scarecrow is crowned King.

The Wizard of Oz (C. Charles Haydon), in the Red Wagon drawn by the Saw-Horse, meets and overcomes Mombi. He puts her in a huge can labeled "Preserved Sandwitches" — then crosses out the "Sand" on the label. Taking the canned witch to King Scarecrow's court, the Wizard makes her agree to melt Gloria's heart so she can love Pon.

There is a confusing number of characters in this film too. Button-Bright, lost as usual, is really not essential. The camera trickery is sometimes highly elementary. To suggest the raft going over a wall of water the camera is tilted first in one direction, then in another. The Wizard shrinks the can to normal can size (on a simple cut in the film). Similarly, he enlarges it toward the end of the story (when, in one shot, the side is cut away to show Mombi cowering within).

However, more elaborate special effects were sometimes required. Mombi is shown taking Gloria's heart and freezing it in her hand before replacing it. In another scene, the Tin Woodman cuts off Mombi's head — and she reaches down and puts it back in place.

The Moving Picture World, a trade journal, summed the film up as "an acceptable offering of entertainment, but more especially for children."

Seen today, these films are of historic interest but of no great artistic value. Perhaps the costuming and makeup of some of the more fantastic characters, like the Tin Woodman and the Woozy, are their strongest features. The limited appeal to adult audiences, which caused their box-office failure, remains evident today.

It would be interesting, though, to see some of the same players in more mature roles in the Oz company's "adult" movie *The Last Egyptian*. J. Farrell MacDonald turned from acting to directing for the drama, and Vivian Reed, Mai Wells and C. Charles Haydon were among those in the cast.

OZ CARRIES ON

□□

The New Royal Historian

Ruth Plumly Thompson with her dog Bob.
[Courtesy of the International Wizard of Oz Club.]

After Baum's death, his publishers conducted a search for a new writer to continue the series. They were particularly impressed by the work of Ruth Plumly Thompson, whose first book of fantasy for children, *The Perhappsy Chaps*, appeared in 1918 from another Chicago publisher. She came from Philadelphia (like Denslow and Neill) and at the time was in her late twenties. Each week a children's page appeared under her name in one of the Philadelphia papers.

Published in 1921, her first Oz work, *The Royal Book of Oz*, maintained the tradition of an annual addition to the series. It was, however, primarily credited to Baum. The publishers described the book as having been "enlarged and edited" by Miss Thompson, as if it had been created from the notes he had left. Oz scholars today consider the book solely her work. John R. Neill continued to provide the illustrations, helping to smooth the transition.

Jack Snow provides a succinct summary of the book in his *Who's Who in Oz*.

Professor Wogglebug lets fall the weighty observation that the Scarecrow has no background — no family tree. So the Scarecrow indignantly goes in search of his family tree to the Munchkin corn field, where he had been placed on a pole long ago to frighten away crows. The pole turns out to be a magic bean pole, and the Scarecrow falls down it, far below the surface of Oz, down to the Silver Islands. Here, the Scarecrow discovers that he is supposed to be the re-created Emperor Chang Wang Woe of the Silver Islands. Among the new characters introduced are: Sir Hokus of Pokes, Comfortable Camel, and Doubtful Dromedary.

Ruth Plumly Thompson had set about expanding the world of Oz. Many now believe it was a mistake to give the Scarecrow such an exalted and improbable position in a former existence. It did explain, though, why he, of all scarecrows in Oz, came to life.

In her second book, the author wrote: "Oz is so large and inhabited by so many strange and singular peoples that although fourteen books of history have been written about it, only half the story has been told." She would reveal the other half.

She went on to write a new book annually until 1940, creating 19 in all, five more than Baum had done. (She also wrote two additional books which the International Wizard of Oz Club published in the 1970s.) According to Jack Snow's survey, she created over 320 new figures in her Oz books, a hundred more than he lists for Baum.

Some of her additions are widely liked. Kabumpo the Elegant Elephant made his debut in her second book and comes from the hitherto unnoticed kingdom of Pumperdink within Oz. In *Kabumpo in Oz*, Miss Thompson also brought back the Nome King, Ruggedo, for another attempt to overthrow Ozma. She enlarges him to a height of three-quarters of a mile and has the Royal Palace of Oz shoot up into the air on his head.

Miss Thompson also elaborated on other aspects of Baum's work. In her 1925 book, *The Lost King of Oz*, she told the story of Pastoria, the former monarch of the fairyland. Baum had mentioned him only in passing, although he had been a character in the stage production of *The Wizard of Oz*. In *The Hungry Tiger of Oz*, she brought to the forefront a subsidiary figure from some earlier books.

Some spelling revisions were made. In *Kabumpo in Oz*, Miss Thompson refers to Gilliken country (rather than Gillikin) and turns the Nomes into Gnomes. The latter is irritating and mistaken. Baum had made it clear, in *Rinkitink in Oz*, that the word "nome" means "one who knows" (one who knows where all the mineral wealth lies in the ground). "Knome" would perhaps have been a more tolerable alteration.

The Royal Palace of Oz impaled on the spikes of the Nome King's giant head in *Kabumpo in Oz*, and the front cover of this 1922 addition to the Oz canon by Ruth Plumly Thompson. [Both courtesy of Contemporary Books Inc., Chicago.]

Miss Thompson's writing style was brisker than Baum's, and she wrote arresting openings. Her adventure stories are more robust, and she favors boy heroes over girls. She is also more enthusiastic, and less idiosyncratic. "There is a capricious quality in the Thompson Oz books that gives them a timbre of fantasy unlike Baum's; this is, I think, their most distinctive characteristic," wrote Russel B. Nye in the Autumn 1965 *Baum Bugle*. She was adept at creating new peoples for the stories. The Figureheads, who are ruled by a Foot Ruler, were her invention. So was the Runaway Island that keeps running around until it can be settled somewhere far enough away to provide a suitable temporary exile for Ruggedo.

The Thompson Oz books bring in a number of foreign elements that for many readers dilute the flavor of Baum's creation. There are echoes of English myth in Sir Hokus of Pokes, a former knight of Merrie England who wants to slay dragons. Overtones of sea-faring romances are found in the figure of the former pirate, Captain Salt. And there is the Orientalism of the Scarecrow's past. For her last book in the annual series, *Ozoplaning in Oz* (1939), she even took the Oz books into the stratosphere.

Of course, Miss Thompson did not write for the sake of posterity. She was content with the fun she had writing the books and with the letters she received from children as the new Royal Historian of Oz. Her publishers were also happy because her new books sold well, and they kept up interest in the older titles. In the mid-1930s, sales of Oz books still reached 100,000 a year.

Scholarly attention has improved Baum's reputation as a writer, and inexpensive paperback editions have brought his books into wide circulation. Yet the works of Ruth Plumly Thompson have not been reprinted, and they have become largely inaccessible and forgotten.

This is about to change. The first six Oz books she wrote were reissued in Spring 1985, in paperback. It will be intriguing to see if her work can enchant modern readers of Baum's books. Perhaps she too will become the subject of serious scrutiny by the literary establishment. She died aged 84 on April 6, 1976.

Left: Ruth Plumly Thompson carried on Baum's practice of replying to young readers' letters while the publisher printed a list of the books in the series on the back of the Royal Historian's notepaper.

The Stories Continue

Ruth Plumly Thompson's voluntary decision to give up writing annual Oz sagas was not the end of the story. John R. Neill stepped up from illustrator to try his hand at writing the books. The result was that the Land of Oz became more incredible than ever.

Neill's first effort, *The Wonder City of Oz* (1940), brings the houses of the Emerald City literally to life. They squabble among themselves, keeping watch for their owners to return and wearing "vacant expressions" if unoccupied.

Neill also devised the spongelike, oily-eyed Heelers, who live off votes and attack the Emerald City in search of them at election time. (Amazingly, Ozma has become a democrat and put herself up for election to continue as ruler of Oz.) The parallels drawn with civic corruption and ward heelers in contemporary America spoil Oz. It should be magical and different, not reminiscent of mundane American life.

In *Lucky Bucky in Oz* (1942), Neill created a wood whale called Davy Jones who is slowly blown across the Magic Rainbow. The Rainbow sags in the middle under his weight. This provides an amusing illustration, but it seems wrong. Either a magic rainbow supports a whale or it doesn't. It can't be half-affected by the laws of gravity.

Neill wrote action-packed narratives and included many puns. Unfortunately, he

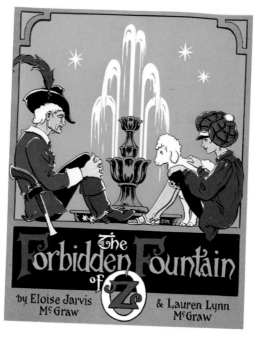

A late addition to the adventures, published in 1980 by the International Wizard of Oz Club and illustrated by Dick Martin.

had no great flair for inventing speech, and his drawing had become a little crude. He no longer provided color work because the use of special pages with full-page color plates had been discontinued some years before.

Lucky Bucky was the last of the three Neill books published before his death in 1943.

A lifelong Oz enthusiast, Jack Snow, wrote two additional books that were closer to Baum's style. He concentrated on the characters Baum had introduced and added only a few of his own.

Rachel R. Cosgrove wrote another book (published in 1951) which added 17 new characters to Jack Snow's *Who's Who In Oz*.

The International Wizard of Oz Club has published three additional Oz books. They include two by Ruth Plumly Thompson who was lured back to Oz after an absence of more than 30 years.

The whale crosses the Rainbow in *Lucky Bucky in Oz* (1942), written and illustrated by John R. Neill. He is being pushed along by the daughters of the Rainbow. Helpful puffs are contributed by four "Gabooches," strange creatures with bellows-shaped heads and strong nozzle-shaped beaks. [Courtesy of Contemporary Books Inc., Chicago.]

NEW FILMS OF OZ

□□□□□□□ □□□□□□□□□□□□□□□□□□□□□□□

The Dud

Oliver Hardy (left) and Larry Semon as two farmhands and romantic rivals for Dorothy Dwan's Dorothy in the 1925 silent version of *The Wizard of Oz*. [Courtesy of the Museum of Modern Art/Film Stills Archive.]

In 1925, one of the more popular screen comedians was Larry Semon. Usually he directed — often he wrote — his own films. At this time, he hit on the idea of turning *The Wizard of Oz* into a vehicle for his brand of silent slapstick comedy. L. Frank Baum Jr. was brought in on the project, and his name appears along with Semon's as one of the three writers.

But Semon had no respect for the original material. He turned Dorothy into a 17-year-old as a role for his brunette wife, Dorothy Dwan. A portly actor called Oliver N. Hardy was cast as his rival for Dorothy's affections. Hardy, a heavy in several of Semon's previous productions, now appeared as a farmhand who sides with the villains.

The resultant movie, *The Wizard of Oz*, at the beginning refers to the original book. As an elderly, stooped figure, Semon is reading the famous story to a small girl. But Semon's subsequent treatment probably offended anyone who loved Baum's work.

A large portion of the film is set on the Kansas farm. There, Semon drops eggs down his pants, is chased by a swarm of bees and is kicked by a mule onto a clump of cactus. He is a shy suitor for Dorothy's affections. Then men arrive from Oz by airplane (!) to try to prevent Dorothy from finding out she is really the Queen of Oz. She will read this in a sealed letter on her 18th birthday explaining why she was left at the farm as a baby.

Discontent is rife in Oz, and Prince Kynd and the people are demanding the return of Dorothy to the throne in place of Prime Minister Kruel. The Wizard of Oz, a sidekick of Kruel's, is instructed to create a diversion. So he produces a phantom creature from a basket (similar to the magical tricks performed by the Wizard in the stage production of the book). Kruel makes the trip to Kansas and bribes a farmhand (Oliver Hardy) to help him.

A handy cyclone whisks Dorothy and others off to Oz, including a black farmhand played by an actor named (no kidding) G. Howe Black. The Wizard is ordered to change the unwelcome farmhands into monkeys, but has to confess "I couldn't change a quarter." To help him fake some magic, Larry Semon substitutes for a scarecrow and then pretends to come to life.

He spends the rest of the picture in scarecrow makeup hiding in boxes and fleeing from lions. Eventually, he is able to help Prince Kynd save Dorothy from marriage to Kruel. Dorothy is grateful but embraces Kynd rather than him. After more chases and the arrival of another airplane, it all turns out to be the little girl's dream.

The Wizard was played by former vaudeville comic and Keystone Kops actor Charlie Murray. (He was also Kelly in the 1930s Cohen and Kelly movies.) His nervous gulps and mugging away at the camera rob the character of dignity. Oliver Hardy has one moment, expressing mock sorrow (that he has chased Larry Semon into a lion's den), which suggests the character he later developed with Stan Laurel. At one point, Hardy falls into a "tin pile" and emerges briefly looking like a tin man. The black actor dons lion's costume to be confused by Semon with a real lion, but there is no Cowardly Lion as in Baum's book.

The film introduced an older, dark-haired Dorothy and farmhands doubling as the Scarecrow and Tin Woodman (to the limited extent these characters are used). It also made Oz a child's dream. But the script was so muddled and uninspired that the film was without merit. Nevertheless, copies of this *Wizard of Oz* film still continue to circulate among movie buffs, solely because of its title and of curiosity about Oliver Hardy as the Tin Woodman.

Oliver Hardy appears very briefly in Tinman costume in the 1925 *Wizard of Oz* film.

The Classic

Metro-Goldwyn-Mayer's classic film *The Wizard of Oz* was first shown to the public in August 1939. Indirectly, Walt Disney was responsible for its being made. Rival studios were convinced Disney's first full-length animated feature, *Snow White and the Seven Dwarfs*, would be a smash hit. Due to open at Christmas 1937, it was expected to create a demand for similar fantasy pictures.

The Oz books were strong sellers. They were some of the most popular American children's books written. So *The Wizard of Oz* was an obvious follow-up. Disney himself had had its availability checked. Sam Goldwyn owned the rights, but he was not interested in filming it.

Goldwyn had bought the book in early 1934 with his contract star Eddie Cantor in mind. He probably envisioned something along the lines of Larry Semon's treatment of the story in the 1925 film. Cantor would perhaps dream himself to Oz in the way he had gone to ancient Rome in *Roman Scandals*, again with the addition of songs. But Cantor's appeal had dwindled, and Goldwyn sold the rights to the highest bidder — MGM — at a tidy profit in 1938.

From the start, MGM pulled out all the stops to do justice to the project. The studio worked hard to produce a film that would appeal to the more discerning and analytical adult audience, as well as to children. The result was a rare instance of a film adapting a fine book sensibly to the screen and subtly improving on it.

As Aljean Harmetz documents in her authoritative book, *The Making of The Wizard of Oz*, no fewer than 10 writers worked on the script as well as three directors. (Those credited in the film were the ones mainly responsible.) Art directors and special effects experts strove to meet the extraordinary demands the subject made on them. As in the case of a cathedral, the result was the work of a *group* of artists working in harmony to a common end.

Judy Garland played Dorothy in the 1939 screen adaptation of *The Wizard of Oz*.
[© 1939 Loew's Incorporated.]

Far left: Dorothy in Munchkinland. Left: the Cowardly Lion (Bert Lahr), the Tin Woodman (Jack Haley) and the Scarecrow (Ray Bolger) confront the humbug Wizard of Oz (Frank Morgan). Below: undated poster. [Scenes: © 1939 Loew's Incorporated. Copyright renewed 1966 by Metro-Goldwyn-Mayer Inc. Poster: courtesy of National Film Archive, London.]

The studio tried to borrow 10-year-old Shirley Temple from 20th Century-Fox to play Dorothy. Eventually, however, MGM selected its own 16-year-old Judy Garland, who convincingly acted below her real age. Her chest was flattened, and initially she was dressed in a blond curly wig to conform to Baum's description, until everyone realized light hair didn't suit her.

The other characters were all ably cast — Ray Bolger as the Scarecrow, Jack Haley as the Tin Woodman and Bert Lahr as the Cowardly Lion. Blustery Frank Morgan made a superb, bulbous-cheeked Wizard (W. C. Fields had turned it down), and Margaret Hamilton had the role of a lifetime playing the Wicked Witch of the West.

Watch Toto carefully, and you can see a remarkably disciplined canine performance. The Munchkins were played by 90 male and 34 female midgets. (MGM had wanted 200. Baum had only three actually greet Dorothy in his book.) The casting of fluttery Billie Burke as the Good Witch Glinda was not so universally admired. Yet her lightheaded manner — even if far from Baum's concept of the character — did suggest a sweet disposition not strong enough to contest the power of the Wicked Witch.

The script did a thorough job of condensing, integrating and generally

The frightening vision that greets Dorothy and her companions on entering the Wizard's inner sanctum in the 1939 movie of *The Wizard of Oz*. [© 1939 Loew's Incorporated. Copyright renewed 1966 by Metro-Goldwyn-Mayer Inc.]

tidying up the original book. Left out of the film were the ferocious beasts the Kalidahs, the Hammerheads and the Dainty China country in the interests of a simpler, cleaner narrative. The Tin Woodman's story and the tale told by the leader of the Winged Monkeys to explain their servitude to the Wicked Witch were both omitted.

Dorothy, the Scarecrow, the Tin Woodman and the Cowardly Lion meet the Wizard as a group, instead of individually. His most awesome appearances from the book, as a giant head and a ball of fire, are combined.

The Wicked Witch of the West appears as an adversary from the beginning of Dorothy's adventure in Oz, trying to obtain the magic slippers. The Witch is associated with the Talking Trees that throw apples at Dorothy and the Scarecrow. She threatens the Scarecrow with a fireball from a rooftop. And it is she who fixes the poppies so they cause drowsiness (for which Baum offered no real explanation). The film adds the visual flourish of the Witch skywriting "Surrender Dorothy" on her broomstick.

In the screen version, Dorothy and the others are ordered by the Wizard to bring him the Witch's broomstick if they want their requests granted. They are not asked to kill her. It is a much more reasonably framed demand to make of the girl, one that she can more plausibly accept. And when Dorothy melts the Witch with water, it is more convincingly arranged. The Witch has set the Scarecrow alight, and Dorothy picks up a bucket of water to put out the fire. Accidentally, she douses the evil crone and (as the Wizard later remarks humorously) "liquidates" her.

The film also turns Dorothy's trip into a dream-nightmare. It is still scary. Even now, the Witch frightens young viewers, and adults shudder decades later at the effect she made. (In Britain, the censor gave it an "A" certificate in 1940, requiring children to be accompanied by an adult.)

However, it can be argued that Baum's marvelous creation of Oz is weakened and trivialized by turning it into a child's

LADIES' HOME JOURNAL

Judy Garland poses with L. Frank Baum's widow and the first edition of the famous story. Picture taken at MGM's studios. The magazine advertisement for the film dates from September 1939.

imaginings. In fact, though, Baum seems attracted to the same explanation, as described earlier. At any rate, the writers go to ingenious lengths in creating a much longer Kansas prologue, with "hooks" to stimulate Dorothy's imagination. Characters are invented that reappear in different guises in Oz, played by the same performers.

The Wicked Witch is suggested by Elvira Gulch, an unpleasant spinster neighbor who obtains a sheriff's order to take away Toto for biting her. (Toto also likes to chase her cat. This ties in with Toto causing Dorothy to miss the balloon flight back to Kansas when he takes off after another cat.) Dorothy runs away from home with Toto but returns after the traveling mind-reader and magician, Professor Marvel, suggests Aunt Em will be worrying about her. Marvel becomes the humbug Wizard of Oz.

Three jovial farmhands become the models for the Scarecrow, Cowardly Lion and Tin Woodman. Hunk, who talks about lack of brains and having a head full of straw, becomes the Scarecrow. Zeke, who speaks of having little courage and is scared when Dorothy falls into a pigsty, is the Cowardly Lion. Hickory poses as a statue, momentarily, with his hands up — exactly as the Tin Woodman is first seen.

Aunt Em, however, only appears in Oz as herself in the Witch's magic ball. She is worrying about Dorothy, just as Professor Marvel claimed to see her in his crystal ball. If she and Uncle Henry were in Oz in any form, it would undermine Dorothy's desire to return home. In this film, life in Kansas (filmed in black and white, and printed originally in sepia) is not as colorful as Oz. It lacks other children, but it is busy and happy enough for Dorothy to want to go back, unlike the gray world of Baum's book.

The farm sequences (directed by King Vidor, without credit) were shot entirely on a sound stage. This was the custom for most scenes in even serious drama, but it is more glaringly obvious today than in

1939. Yet the artificiality of the film's depiction of Kansas now usefully narrows the gap between it and Oz. Elvira Gulch would be unbelievable cycling along real roads.

It is the use of vivid Technicolor for the Land of Oz that first distinguishes it from Kansas. With it MGM ensured maximum impact was achieved, right down to changing the magic slippers from silver to ruby so they stood out better. The color even contributes to a visual pun on the phrase "horse of a different color" in the *art deco*-styled Emerald City.

The opening title reads, "For nearly 40 years this story has given faithful service to the Young in Heart; and Time has been powerless to put its kindly philosophy out of fashion." Some people consider that the point of the film — that we should look inside ourselves for qualities we are seeking — is over-stressed.

Glinda actually asks what Dorothy has learned at the end. The answer she gets is "I think that it wasn't enough just to want to see Uncle Henry and Aunt Em. And that it's if I ever go looking for my heart's desire again, I won't look any further than my own backyard because if it isn't there I never really lost it in the first place." Expressed more generally in her closing remark, "Oh, Aunt Em, there's no place like home!", it is a sentiment to which not everyone would subscribe. (Baum uses the expression much earlier in his book, which concludes with the less succinct phrasing "And oh, Aunt Em! I'm so glad to be at home again!")

The film shows Dorothy waking up from her dream, surrounded by her caring family and friends (even Professor Marvel looks in). Conveniently, the unresolved matter of the sheriff's order to seize Toto, which earlier caused Dorothy to run away, is not mentioned.

The film was modeled on the Denslow drawings but drew also from the book's history as a musical comedy. This gave a precedent for the use of musical numbers. The Oz songs by Harold Arlen and E.Y. Harburg are all fun and inventive — *We're Off to See the Wizard, The Merry Old Land*

of Oz, the Munchkins' number *Ding-Dong! The Witch Is Dead* and others. The one serious number — Judy Garland's solo *Over the Rainbow*, with its innocent yearning for another world — is placed in Kansas before the introduction of color and the fantastic settings of Oz.

The stage *Wizard of Oz* is the source of the snowfall that arouses Dorothy in the poppy field. (In the film, the snow is attributed to Glinda's intervention.) That version is also heavily echoed in Bert Lahr's Cowardly Lion from his first appearance. His paws become fists as he brandishes them, roaring "Put 'em up, put 'em up! Which one of you foist?" — a vaudeville approach that seems rather out of place in Oz.

There is a weak link in the film. It occurs when the Scarecrow, Tin Man and Lion overpower the Wicked Witch's guards to steal their uniforms and are chased around the castle by more of her men. The inspiration momentarily sags here. It is amusing, though to notice the guards all have pointed, prominent noses, like their mistress.

In its efforts to produce as smooth a film as possible, MGM even cut two elaborate musical sequences. There was the *Jitter Bug* number, in which pink and blue bugs attacked Dorothy and friends in the forest on the way to the Wicked Witch. There was also the *Renovation Sequence* of Dorothy's return in triumph to the Emerald City with the burnt broomstick.

Other cuts included a sequence of Ray Bolger's Scarecrow dancing in the air (on wires). This dance footage survives and is included in the 1985 MGM compilation film *That's Dancing!* In addition, film of the *Jitter Bug* number being shot was recently shown on television.

The Wizard of Oz went over budget, costing altogether $2,777,000 to make. It was popular with audiences (less so with critics), but it still lost money on its first release. The war in Europe reduced its potential earnings. Still, MGM considered making a sequel in the early 1940s. In 1940, 20th Century-Fox released a rival fantasy film, *The Blue Bird* with Shirley Temple, that was a box-office disaster.

The story lives on. Poster for a British pantomime production that ran from Dec. 17, 1976 to Feb. 5, 1977.
[Courtesy of Birmingham Repertory Theatre.]

There never was a great cycle of fantasy films. Only *Dr Cyclops* and *The Thief of Bagdad* turned up in 1940, in addition to Disney's animated *Pinocchio* and *Fantasia*, and Fox's *The Blue Bird*.

Of course, the MGM film's enduring appeal is twofold. It had the magic of Oz and also the magic of Judy Garland. Her performance is consistently superb. Open-eyed, amused, frightened, indignant, finally wise, she is a touching, thoroughly convincing Dorothy. She was not a star when she made the film. She had first billing but was listed with all the other players. *The Wizard of Oz* made her famous. It also won her a special Academy Award for an outstanding performance by a screen juvenile, the only Oscar she ever had. Her tragic life lends poignancy now to her youthful singing of *Over the Rainbow*.

The MGM film has almost entirely by itself sustained the interest in Baum's books. They are measured against the impression left by the film — not the other way around. The movie even stirred up new interest in stage productions. It prompted the first production of the Baum-Tietjens play in Britain, at the Grand Theatre in Croydon, over Christmas 1942. MGM licensed the use of their script and songs for another British adaptation by Janet Green, which opened in the West End of London during Christmas 1947. (There has been a steady stream of presentations of various versions at British provincial theaters ever since, as well as numerous amateur productions.)

UPLIFTERS OF OZ

1957 – The Club

Over the years, several Oz clubs have been established. The publishers of the Oz books promoted children's fan clubs in the 1920s with free pins and a free "newspaper," *The Ozmapolitan*. Other spontaneous groups of devotees also formed. But in 1957 the first serious lasting association of Oz enthusiasts was formed at the instigation of Justin G. Schiller, a Brooklyn teenager.

He produced the first issue of *The Baum Bugle*, consisting of four mimeographed pages, for the benefit of 16 founder members. Today the group has grown into the thriving International Wizard of Oz Club, Inc.

By the 1950s, public interest in the Baum books had declined. But two developments took place in 1956 that helped change all that. The first Baum book, *The Wizard of Oz*, had passed into the public domain. Various new editions, sometimes abridgments, sometimes with new illustrations, began to appear, often as inexpensive paperbacks. The film, *The Wizard of Oz*, made its debut on television at the end of 1956, and so began its extraordinary career as a potent audience puller.

And the International Wizard of Oz Club was there to help those who wanted to know more about Oz and its creators. By 1985, its membership totaled 1,925, and in 1984 the 80th issue of *The Baum Bugle* appeared. An annual gathering of members, called the Ozmapolitan Convention, began in 1961 and has often been held at Castle Park, Michigan. It is an area where Baum spent many summers amidst a fairylike atmosphere of tall trees, emerald-green lawns and a castle.

Munchkin conventions were established for members in the east. Displays, quizzes, costume contests, play performances and film screenings are featured. Similar Winkie conventions have been held in the west for members living there.

The Club can be contacted care of Fred M. Meyer, 220 North 11th Street, Escanaba, MI 49829.

Shirley Temple in Oz

Shirley Temple would have played Dorothy in MGM's *The Wizard of Oz* if 20th Century-Fox had been prepared to loan her out. Finally, though, she did find her way to Baum's fairyland.

In 1958, she began presenting children's tales on television in a program called *The Shirley Temple Storybook*. On Sunday September 18, 1960, she inaugurated a new hour-long series called *The Shirley Temple Show*. Its first broadcast was a taped adaptation of the second Oz book, *The Land of Oz*.

The time available wasn't long enough to do justice to the story, but the writer still introduced some new characters. There was a villainous Nikidik (played by Jonathan Winters), attended by his gloating butler (veteran character actor Arthur Treacher).

Shirley Temple appeared as a blond-wigged Tip. She was more than just following pantomime tradition in playing a boy's part because he is transformed into Princess Ozma at the end. The actress was then able to appear as her normal, radiant self. Even so, some contemporary adult observers felt the sex change was distasteful for family viewing!

Apart from Jack Pumpkinhead and the Saw-Horse, audiences also met the Scarecrow, Tin Woodman and Glinda from the first story of Oz. But the most striking performance came from Agnes Moorehead, who played the witch Mombi to perfection, employing a derisive manner and a Cockney accent. (It helped her win the part for which she later became most widely known — the cantankerous mother-in-law witch Endora in the long-running television series, *Bewitched*.)

Two covers from the magazine of the International Wizard Oz Club. One shows L Frank Baum, the othe the Oz characters as drawn by Riu Yamaza for a 1976 Japanese version of the first Oz book, *Ozu no Mahotsukai*. This issu of the *Bugle* updated their listing of Japane: editions. [Courtesy of the International Wizard of Oz Club.]

LATER SCREEN AND STAGE PRODUCTIONS

Animated Oz

In 1960 and 1961, television used the Oz characters for a series of 5-minute cartoons shown on Saturday mornings. Called *Tales of the Wizard of Oz*, the cartoons were made by the Arthur Rankin Jr.–Jules Bass organization, which also produced *Return to Oz* to fill an hour slot in 1963.

Return to Oz included numerous chirpy, but rather forgettable, songs. The animation was elementary, with much use of plain colors and geometric lines. The film purported to show Dorothy making a second trip to Oz, but it was really the original story again with some cheapening changes.

Another Kansas twister whips Dorothy and Toto off to Oz as they cling to an apple tree. She drops into Munchkinland and is acclaimed by the Munchkins and given the chocolate key to the city. (The Munchkins are all different colors instead of being dressed only in blue.)

Glinda materializes and has some alarming news for Dorothy. The Wicked Witch of the West has recovered from the meltdown and gained temporary magical powers from a cousin, the Wretched Witch of the Wastelands. It is the Witch who has whisked Dorothy back in the hope of stealing her silver slippers (which she evidently didn't lose on her way home last time). The Witch believes the slippers will give her real powers, but she doesn't know that anyone using them who is heartless, cowardly or brainless will turn to stone.

[Courtesy of National Film Archive, London.]

Dorothy finds her old friends Socrates, Rusty and Dandy. *Who?* These are the "improved" names for the Scarecrow, the Tin Woodman and the Cowardly Lion. The Witch has tricked them all, burning Socrates' diploma, melting Rusty's heart and turning Dandy's medal into a daisy. They again demand real brains, heart and courage from the Wizard who is still operating his fire-breathing head. And they are told to capture the Wicked Witch all over again.

After braving her lightning bolts and flying reptiles, they finally surrender the slippers to the Witch because she has Dorothy in her clutches. The old hag turns to stone. Glinda appears to make sure we've understood the "message" of the story. Rusty has shown love, Socrates displayed quick thinking, and Dandy was courageous in tackling the Witch. She, meanwhile, has paid the penalty for being "heartless as anyone is who is cruel, cowardly as anyone is who must use slaves and suppress others, and brainless as

Three images (not available in color) from *Journey Back to Oz*. Shown are Dorothy and Jack Pumpkinhead, the Yellow Brick Road, and Mombi on one of her army of elephants.
[Courtesy of National Film Archive, London.]

The Scarecrow and the Tin Woodman as created by Bil Baird for his puppet production of *The Wizard of Oz* (1968). [Courtesy of Bil Baird.]

anyone is who thinks evil can conquer good." The moral is quite a mouthful!

Dorothy told us at the start, in her cute fashion, "Stay away from Kansas too long and I get homesick." Now she wishes hard for some Kansas-style magic, and a cyclone returns her to Aunt Em and Uncle Henry.

The movie is not very entertaining, but it is amazing. The script plays on knowledge of the original story, yet recreates it so feebly that anyone with an ounce of the Scarecrow's — or Socrates' — brains would be offended.

A far more elaborate animated tale of the Land of Oz, again with songs, was made in the 1960s. It was not released until several years later, and was entitled *Journey Back to Oz*. The film recruited some distinguished names to voice the characters, including Margaret Hamilton who this time played Aunt Em instead of the Wicked Witch. For Dorothy, the filmmakers used Judy Garland's daughter, Liza Minnelli, whose careful speech shows great respect for the part (it was also her first professional assignment). There was another reminder of Judy in the casting of her old co-star Mickey Rooney to speak the lines of the Scarecrow. Other celebrated names included Ethel Merman as the witch Mombi and Milton Berle as the Cowardly Lion.

Once again Dorothy and Toto are whirled away to Oz by a cyclone. In Oz, they set out for the Emerald City where the Scarecrow is now king. Dorothy meets Pumpkinhead and learns Mombi is plotting to overthrow the Scarecrow and become queen. Joined by Woodenhead the Horse, they are chased by Mombi and her army of magic green elephants into the City, which soon falls into the witch's hands.

Dorothy escapes and finds the Tin Man and Cowardly Lion too afraid to help. "Courage is not enough, you've got to have nerve," laments the Lion in one of the musical numbers. Then Dorothy calls on Glinda to help her, and is told to have faith in herself. She also receives a magic box for emergency use. Later, when surrounded by the elephants, she opens it to release a horde of mice who cause a stampede. Mombi transforms herself into a rose to escape capture but is trampled by elephants. Peace is restored to Oz, and Dorothy decides to go back to Kansas.

Drawing its inspiration chiefly from the second Oz book, *The Land of Oz*, the film makes some drastic changes. Dorothy is worked into the story, which invents the elephants as well as a talking Signpost. The character animation is comparatively uninteresting although the backgrounds are good.

In 1967, the celebrated animator Chuck Jones turned his hand to visualizing Oz with *Off to See the Wizard*. This was a series of prologues in which the Wizard was represented as selecting feature films for his friends in Oz to view. It was a way to dress up a season of movies to be more interesting for families to watch.

The veteran puppeteer Bil Baird created an acclaimed production of *The Wizard of Oz* in 1968. It used songs from the 1939 movie but was otherwise Baird's own version of the story. Opening in New York on November 27, 1968, it ran until March 2, 1969. Regrettably, no film or television record seems to have been made of the show.

During this period, an obscure live-action feature was released. Again based on the second Oz book, *The Wonderful Land of Oz* played theaters beginning in 1969. It worked Dorothy (plus a purple cow) into the story and packed eight songs into its brief 72-minute running time. By all evidence, it was a very minor effort.

Black Oz

The successful stage revival of *Hello, Dolly!* in the early 1970s with an all-black cast was influential in several ways. One was to trigger a search for other tested material that could be given a new lease on life in the same way.

Kenneth Harper, a young black disc jockey in New York City, hit on the idea of an all-black *Wizard of Oz*. It would be based on Baum's original book instead of the MGM movie. Lyricist and composer Charlie Smalls wrote some sample songs and Harper sought backing for a Broadway show. It was a time when some Hollywood studios were investing in Broadway in the hope of nurturing future movie hits. 20th Century-Fox liked Harper's proposal enough to put up $650,000 to back the production.

It was called *The Wiz*, and it tried out in Baltimore in October 1974. The director was Gilbert Moses III, with the book written by William F. Brown, costumes designed by Geoffrey Holder, choreography by George Faison, and songs by Charlie Smalls. *Variety's* reviewer deemed it "a sick patient with good prospects for a healthy future." Numerous changes were made, including Geoffrey Holder being named the director. He introduced the Tornado ballet and eliminated other things, including the veteran character actress Butterfly McQueen's role as Queen of the Field Mice.

The Wiz opened on Broadway on January 5, 1975, at the Majestic. This was not the same Majestic Theater at which *The Wizard of Oz* had opened in 1902 (that had been demolished) but the later one on West 45th Street. "The all-black, jazzed-up rock-music edition of the old L. Frank Baum yarn is done with great gusto," reported "Hobe" in *Variety*. He also referred to "ear-splitting amplification" and "contagiously enthusiastic" dancing. It

The 1975 New York stage production of *The Wiz*: Charles Valentino as the Scarecrow, Ken Prymus as the Lion, Renee Harris as Dorothy and Ben Harney as the Tin Man with dancers representing the yellow brick road. [© 1975 Martha Swope.]

□ □

The black musical version of *The Wizard of Oz* lives on. Poster designed by the Drawing Room for a British revival from Dec. 8, 1984 to Feb. 2, 1985.
[Courtesy of the Lyric Theatre, Hammersmith, London.]

The Scarecrow, Dorothy, the Lion and the Tin Man in the 1975 stage hit, *The Wiz*.
[© 1975 Martha Swope.]

was cheered by black audiences. In time, regular theater-goers came and liked what they saw, making it a fashionable show to see.

The Wiz takes a refreshingly cool attitude toward the original story. It assumes basic audience familiarity with the characters and quickly works away from the traditional Kansas farmyard opening. A cynical urban environment is shown in which the Emerald City is "the Big Green Apple," and skyscrapers abound. The Gatekeeper will let anyone in for a bribe. The Wicked Witch of the West, now called Evillene, is queen of a gambling den. The Scarecrow steps out of an advertizing billboard and the Cowardly Lion is an effeminate figure in a Lions' football costume. The Wizard travels by helicopter.

Dorothy is still a wide-eyed innocent. By the end of the play, she has the best of both worlds. She goes home, *and* she keeps the slippers (silver, as in the original book) so she can return to her new friends in Oz any time.

The tornado and the yellow brick road are represented by dancers, carrying yellow sticks with pointing hands to guide Dorothy on her way. There is plenty of scope for stage spectacle, in raising the farmhouse off the ground (by wires) and elevating the Wiz's helicopter for its takeoff. A recent British production threw in some laser effects to accentuate the action. But it is the energetic dancing and the powerful beat of the music that account for this play's success.

Filming *The Wiz*

Even though 20th Century-Fox under the name CinemaScope Products had backed *The Wiz* on Broadway, it declined to make the movie. Executive changes at the studio had been made, and recent musical bombs — *Doctor Dolittle, Star!* and even *Hello, Dolly!* — prompted caution. A film version of *The Wiz* had to appeal to more than the established black audience to make a profit, and that was by no means certain.

Motown recording company was interested in taking over the project, and worked out a deal for Universal Pictures to acquire the rights. Motown had had two movie hits with Diana Ross in *Lady Sings the Blues* and *Mahogany*. So when she expressed an interest in playing Dorothy, it appeared to guarantee the success of the film. It also encouraged a larger budget.

Sidney Lumet, a respected director

based in New York, was hired to direct the film. It would be his first musical. A new script was written by Joel Schumacher. Lumet, Schumacher and production designer Tony Walton worked out a visual scheme for the film. Production began in September 1977.

The Wiz ended up costing $24 million, way over budget, owing to technical and weather problems and union difficulties. It was the second most expensive film released in 1978. (*Superman* was the most expensive.)

In the film version, the story opens in New York City. Diana Ross's Dorothy is a shy, retiring 24-year-old kindergarten teacher living in Harlem. She has never been south of 125th Street. She is urged by her Aunt Em to start teaching older children and to find a place of her own. A

The Wizard once again appears in the form of an awesome giant head to Dorothy and her companions in the film version of *The Wiz* (1978). [Copyright © by Universal Pictures, a Division of Universal City Studios, Inc. Courtesy of MCA Publishing Rights, a Division of MCA Inc.]

new song written for the film, *Can I Go On Not Knowing?*, eloquently voices her fear of taking a chance. It is snowing outside, and Toto is loose. Dorothy goes after him and is whisked away by a tornado to a Land of Oz that is a harsh parody of New York.

New York City can look attractive if filmed in the right way. But here it is shown at its worst — cold and hostile. Landmarks like the Chrysler Building, the World Trade Center and the New York Public Library are pressed into service, but without affection. The yellow of the Yellow Brick Road is harsh and glaring. (There is *some* updating that works. The Winged Monkeys are now Flying Monkeys on motorbikes, and the Wicked Witch of the West runs a sweatshop.)

What was light, airy, stylized and fantastic in the stage version becomes ponderous and too specific here. There is a greater attempt to follow the original story line — but it just won't transfer to that degree in a metropolitan setting. What is a scarecrow doing on urban wasteland? Or a cowardly lion (in traditional costume) in a city? The attempt to make a subway station the equivalent of the Fighting Trees — gleaming white-tiled columns and snapping trash bins advance on Dorothy and her companions — is embarrassingly awkward. The Wiz is back with his hot-air balloon rather than a helicopter.

The costumes of the Scarecrow, Tinman and Lion smother the actors, although Michael Jackson's Scarecrow has some affecting moments. Sidney Lumet's celebrated skill with actors ensures that

Diana Ross makes a fine Dorothy, believably timid and slowly gaining confidence. Vocally, she is splendid, especially when Dorothy imparts confidence to her friends (*Believe in Yourself*) and is ready to return (*Home*, sung facing the camera). She joins in the dancing with both skill and abandon.

The only traditionally-conceived sequences are those that show Lena Horne as Glinda, floating in starry space like the old-fashioned Hollywood concept of Heaven. This can be criticized as incompatible with the rest of the picture (as can Miss Horne's overpowering rendition of *Believe in Yourself*).

The heart of Baum's story is still there — that people must find in themselves what they are searching for. Here, the uninviting nature of Oz makes Dorothy's willingness to kill Evillene and her desire to go home fully understandable despite the friendships she has developed with the Scarecrow, Tinman and Cowardly Lion.

The film suggests that Glinda whisked Dorothy out of Harlem to make her stand on her own two feet. "Dorothy, you were wise and good enough to help your friends find what was inside them all the time. That's true for you also," Glinda tells her. And she goes on to explain, "Home is a place we must all find, child. It's not just a place where you eat or sleep. Home is knowing — knowing your mind, your heart, your courage. If we know ourselves, we're always home anywhere."

Lena Horne persuasively stretches the word "home" to mean "self-confidence." After all, home — with Aunt Em in Harlem — is the last place, for the sake of her future growth, this Dorothy should go. Even if only a temporary return is meant, it is perhaps typical of this misguided film that its last image should be of Dorothy going home.

The Wiz was quite successful with audiences, even though it lost money. There was an immediate audience for Diana Ross and the lively music of the movie. But the wider audience must have suspected that the film lacked enchantment, and they stayed away. This movie had little to do with the Oz that people knew and loved.

☐☐☐☐☐☐☐☐☐☐☐☐☐☐☐☐☐☐☐
And Oz Down Under

Graham Matters as the Wizard and Joy Dunstan as Dorothy in the 1976 modern Australian color adaptation of *The Wizard of Oz* called *Oz* in its country of origin and *20th Century Oz* for American release.
[Courtesy of National Film Archive, London.]

The Wiz was not the only attempt to refashion the out-of-copyright material in the book *The Wizard of Oz* to suit contemporary tastes. In the early 1970s, Chris Lofven, a young film-maker and former rock musician from another "Oz", Australia, began to plan a new version. It was to be a down-under road movie with a rock background. He called his film *Oz* and shot it around Melbourne on a shoestring budget in 1976.

It is quite an ingenious reworking of the familiar tale, even if it does not appeal to everyone. A 16-year-old blond, Dorothy is a groupie traveling with a four-piece band when she is involved in a road accident. Knocked unconscious she imagines she is on her own, hitchhiking to the city to catch the final concert of a rock superstar, the Wizard. A pair of red shoes in the window of a boutique called The Good Fairy strongly attracts her.

On the road she meets the spaced-out, gentle "surfie" — Australian for "surfer" — named Blondie, likable but not very bright . . . like the Scarecrow. She also encounters Killer, a cowardly biker (or "bikie", as the Australians say) in black leather. He greets her in a service station toilet with lines that echo Bert Lahr's Cowardly Lion in the 1939 film, and bursts into tears when threatened. And Greaseball — he's an auto mechanic who couldn't care less about other people — until he gets to know Dorothy. And he finds — like the Tin Woodman — he has a heart.

Dorothy is pursued by a huge trucker (or "truckie") but her new friends courageously save her from rape by this equivalent of the Wicked Witch. Eventually, Dorothy manages to meet the Wizard but is severely disappointed. The lesson is that fame spoils people.

Australian singer/songwriter Ross Wilson provided the rock score, which was recorded live during shooting. Most Australian critics apparently loathed the film with its crude humor and deafening soundtrack. It spoiled their memories of the 1939 movie. The film was not a commercial success, but it had its defenders. One of them was the respected middle-aged critic David Stratton who later wrote, in his 1980 book *The Last Wave,*

Oz is one of the most inventive and enjoyable of Australian films — clever, brash, noisy, gutsy and uninhibited. Affectionate in its transposition of *The Wizard of Oz* to Australia, it is infinitely preferable to Sidney Lumet's lumpish and garish film version of *The Wiz* (1978). The concept of Dorothy as a persistent little groupie who fends off incipient rape on the highways of Victoria so as to sleep with the greatest rock star of all is an ingenious one, and her final realisation that "fame really f–s you up" is a marvellously cynical '70s variation on the original Dorothy's realisation that "there's no place like home." One dreads to think what *this* Dorothy's home would have been like. All the players, including the inexperienced Joy Dunstan, are excellent and all in all *Oz* is one of the most intelligent teenage-oriented rock musicals ever made.

It played in American movie theaters as *20th Century Oz* in 1977. For that release, the music was re-mixed into four-track stereo and 12 minutes were eliminated by the director to tighten it up.

RIPPLES FROM OZ

□ □

Oz Inspires Writers . . .

Apart from inspiring *The Wiz*, Baum's Oz stories have stimulated a wide range of science-fiction authors, popular musicians and film-makers.

An early instance is Ray Bradbury's 1951 short story, *The Exiles*. In it, Baum's books, in addition to the works of Charles Dickens and Edgar Allan Poe, are taken by rocket to Mars to escape the bookburners who would destroy their visions forever on Earth. (Bradbury later contributed the preface, entitled "Because, Because, Because, Because of the Wonderful Things He Does," to the 1974 academic book on Baum's work, *Wonderful Wizard, Marvelous Land*.)

In his 1964 novel *Glory Road*, Robert A. Heinlein took his heroes along a yellow brick road into other worlds. The same author's 1980 novel *The Number of the Beast* features its four leading characters in an Oz that is much like the one described by Baum. So much so they are not allowed to indulge in sexual activities — by order of Glinda!

Keith Laumer's *The Other Side of Time* (1965) presents a hero who slips into an alternative world that diverged from our own in 1814. He finds a book by L. Frank Baum called *The Sorceress of Oz*, published in 1896 with illustrations by W.W. Denslow. It is Baum's only work in this other world because he is supposed to have died a year after publication. In this alternative world, its story of Sorana the Sorceress in the Sapphire City became a children's classic, whereas *The Wizard of Oz* is unknown.

Perhaps the most startling use of Oz occurs in Philip José Farmer's *A Barnstormer in Oz* (1982). This novel supposes that a real Dorothy was transported to Oz from the Dakota Territory at the time L. Frank Baum was running his newspaper in the town of Aberdeen. Dorothy returns after 6 months and, finding no one believes where she has been, pretends she has become delirious. Baum visits her and

Cover art by Don Ivan Punchatz showing Glinda, the Scarecrow and the Tin Woodman for Philip José Farmer's recent novel. [Courtesy of Berkley Publishing Corporation.]

much later bases *The Wizard of Oz* on what she tells him, adding numerous changes to make it suitable for children.

In Philip José Farmer's account, all Baum's later books were complete fiction. Dorothy has a son, Hank, who knows about her visit to Oz. In April 1923, Hank is a 22-year-old barnstorming pilot who flies into a green cloud — and lands in Oz. There he meets the real Glinda, the Scarecrow and Tin Woodman. Oz is faced with two threats. One is from American experiments that threaten contact with Oz. To this Glinda responds by causing the death of President Harding as a warning to the government to desist. The other threat is from an evil young witch, Erakna, who has seized power in the north of Oz and is poised to invade Glinda's domain in the south.

Farmer confronts many of the apparent absurdities of Oz, such as a living Scarecrow, and his explanations are ingenious. Most Oz devotees would probably prefer the fairyland Baum created without Farmer's detailed introduction of sex and violence. But *A Barnstormer in Oz* is still a tribute to the power of the original books in provoking such a far-ranging reinterpretation.

Oz Inspires Musicians . . .

Pop musicians have also been influenced by Baum's books. The film of *The Wizard of Oz* inspired chart-making revivals of *Somewhere Over the Rainbow* (by the Demensions, 1960) and *Ding Dong! The Witch Is Dead* (by the Fifth Estate, 1967). Elton John's *Goodbye Yellow Brick Road* (No. 2 in November 1973) is the best-known example.

There is also an album called *World of Oz*, composed and performed by a British group of the same name in 1969. The cover artist provides a colorful rendering of Baum's Oz with a rainbow, a blond Dorothy in silver slippers, a Hammerhead and a rainbow. The musicians, on the other hand, give us a Hum Gum Tree, a girl called Mandy Ann and a King Croesus made of stone!

In the 1970 album, *Don McLean Tapestry*, Don McLean includes his own song *Magdalene Lane*, a view of Oz in a state of rotten decay. It refers to MGM's auction of Judy Garland's ruby slippers among other effects in May 1970 and a world where "Aunt Em's on relief and the tinman's a thief/And even the wizard can't wake the dead."

Sleeve design by David Anstey for the 1969 album of numbers by the now disbanded British group, The World of Oz. [© 1969 The Decca Record Company Limited, London. Courtesy of Barry Fishman.]

And Oz Inspires Film-Makers

The appeal of Oz has also been echoed in the movies. Directors of the new generation have had the freedom to make films their way, instead of having to please studio bosses. And they have often quoted images that have been in their minds since childhood.

In *Alice Doesn't Live Here Anymore* (1974), the prologue shows 8-year-old Alice skipping and singing in her Monterey backyard. Her dream is to be a performer "just as good as Alice Faye." Director Martin Scorsese insisted this scene be filmed on the sound stage with ruddy sunset hues in Technicolor at its richest. It looks obviously unreal. The scene is reminiscent of the opening of *The Wizard of Oz* film, in which Judy Garland's Dorothy vocalized her yearnings in much the same way. In contrast, Scorsese shot the adult Alice's experiences on Arizona locations in unobtrusive ordinary color.

In this film, the prologue is the fantasy — the sugarcoated recollection of childhood and the equivalent of Oz. It belongs in lush, exaggerated color to distinguish it from the rest of the movie, which is concerned with mundane reality.

George Lucas could have had something of Baum's books in the back of his mind when he made *Star Wars* (1977). The two Droids are like new versions of the Tin Woodman and Tik-Tok. See-Threepio is a tall figure made of metallic parts, like the Tin Woodman. But he is more nervous and excitable than his Oz counterpart. The short Artoo-Detoo, although he speaks only in whistles and bleeps, is as easily immobilized by falling on his side as Tik-Tok was.

Carrie Fisher's Princess Leia is the equivalent of Princess Ozma, strong on duty and determination. She looks like a fairytale princess, with old-fashioned buns of hair over her ears and her chest flattened (as happened to Judy Garland as Dorothy). But Princess Leia is no pacifist — she jumps into action for her beliefs.

functions are to collect grain from the Brutals and to supply guns to the Exterinators, the overseers who keep the Brutals under control.

One of the Exterminators, Zed (played by Sean Connery), realizes Zardoz is a manmade invention when he spots a copy of *The Wonderful Wizard of Oz* in a dusty, abandoned library. He stows away in the head and confronts its controller and "voice." As a personal vision of John Boorman, the movie is complex and extremely difficult to follow. Much of it baffles even its ardent admirers.

In the British film, *Time Bandits* (1981), another large, disembodied head appears. It contains an old man (played by Sir Ralph Richardson) who is the Supreme Being. Its Munchkinlike group of dwarfs, its child hero and its real-world frame (with characters who appear again in the fantasy) are other reminders of Oz. Actually, it is a cynical comedy in the style of Monty Python.

The film's equivalent of Dorothy is the English schoolboy Kevin. He only becomes an orphan at the end, when his greedy, materialistic parents burn to death before his eyes in their home. Kevin is left with literally "no place like home."

Perhaps the oddest of all films to be dependent on Oz is *Under the Rainbow* (1981). It is a comedy that is supposed to be based on the little people playing the Munchkins in 1938 while making MGM's *The Wizard of Oz*. Legend has it that the activities of the little people in the hotel where they were billeted were lively, to put it mildly. However, this film also throws in Japanese agents and an assassin.

Mainly slapstick, it stars Carrie Fisher as the Munchkins' den mother, Chevy Chase as a special agent and Eve Arden as a duchess whose life is in danger. Also featured are Billy Barty, Pat McCormick and Adam Arkin. One chase scene is set inside the MGM studio and interrupts the shooting of several pictures in production on the lot.

The central symbol of *Zardoz* (1974) is the huge stone head that gives the film its title. It keeps the ordinary Brutals under control in the year 2293. [Poster: courtesy of the National Film Archive, London. Scene still: courtesy of 20th Century-Fox.]

Chewbacca the Wookie is perhaps a nod toward the Cowardly Lion, and Darth Vader is an update of the Wicked Witch, while (to stretch the analogy) Obi-Wan Kenobi is a reclusive Wizard who does help when asked and isn't a humbug.

At any rate, there is no mistaking the homage to the *Wizard of Oz* film in the highly successful *Gremlins* (1984). There, Elvira Gulch is recreated in the form of Mrs. Teagle (played by Polly Holliday). Mrs. Teagle not only has the appearance and manner of Miss Gulch, but she is also intent on doing something nasty and final to the leading youngster's pet dog who, like Toto, has been annoying her cats. However, when she flies through the air, it is not as a wicked witch but as a victim of the mischievous gremlins.

The huge head the Wizard of Oz manipulated to frighten visitors has also loomed large in two films. John Boorman's *Zardoz* (1974), shot in Ireland, even uses a title derived from "Wizard of Oz." It is set in the year 2293, following the collapse of industrial society. At that time scientists and intellectuals have established themselves as Eternals in the Vortex, a commune set in a rich, verdant valley. Outside the Vortex, in the polluted wasteland known as the Outlands, live the Brutals who are slaves of the Eternals.

A trickster named Arthur Frayn is given the task of controlling the Outlands and, inspired by *The Wizard of Oz* book, he creates a god called Zardoz. Zardoz is in the shape of a huge stone head that is powered for flight and is feared and respected by the Brutals. Its practical

DISNEY AND OZ

As mentioned earlier, Walt Disney had been interested in *The Wizard of Oz* as a follow-up to *Snow White and the Seven Dwarfs*, but MGM beat him to the movie rights. Disney's interest in Oz was revived in the 1950s when the studio was active in films and television. On November 16, 1954, Disney bought the rights to 11 of the later books by Baum, adding the other two (held by other producers) in 1956.

As Disney archivist David R. Smith has recorded, the studio's original plan was for a two-part *Disneyland* show on television, drawn largely from *The Patchwork Girl of Oz*. However, it would have been too expensive for the home screen. So a big-budget live-action musical feature, to be called *The Rainbow Road to Oz*, was announced in July 1957. The stars would be television Mouseketeers, such as Annette Funicello and Darlene Gillespie.

To test the concept, two musical numbers were inexpensively filmed and shown on the *Disneyland Fourth Anni-* *versary Show* on September 11, 1957. One number was a song called *Patches*, featuring the first meeting of the Patchwork Girl and the Scarecrow on the yellow brick road. The Scarecrow picks patches from a tree to mend her dress. The second concerned the Oz-Kan Hop, a dance that is partly Kansas, partly Oz. In it, the Cowardly Lion has become a cruel, conceited King of Oz. Dorothy, Ozma and others try to break the spell that has transformed him.

Disney himself appeared on the show and approved their efforts, making it clear the film project had been given the go-ahead. And yet a few months later it was dropped. Various factors must have

Disneyland Fourth Anniversary Show (1957). Far left: the Cowardly Lion on the throne of Oz. Above: the *Patches* number. Left: Walt Disney's appearance on the show holding the script for the planned *The Rainbow Road to Oz*.

84

played a part. There were probably fears about the high cost and the unproven big screen appeal of the television stars. Above all, there may have been worry over unfavorable comparisons with *The Wizard of Oz* after it had begun reaching huge new audiences on the home screen. Judy Garland was too old to play Dorothy again but dare anyone else play her while Garland was still alive?

The studio gave occasional thought to an Oz film when reviewing its inventory of story material. Nothing more happened until 1981, when the company was recruiting new talent to direct movies for them. An approach was made to Walter Murch, an editor, writer and sound designer who had won an Oscar for the soundtrack of *Apocalypse Now*.

Murch had been a devotee of the Baum Oz books since childhood. In the early 1970s, he had watched the Muppets on television and felt they had affinities with some of the Oz characters. He also felt that the techniques used on the show raised new possibilities for making an Oz film. Mentioning the idea to Disney executives, it was only then that he discovered Disney Studios already held the rights. The result was the large-scale Disney production, *Return to Oz*, released in the summer of 1985.

The Coronation procession from *Return to Oz* (1985) in which numerous additional Oz figures join the main characters.
[© Walt Disney Productions.]

85

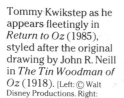

Tommy Kwikstep as he appears fleetingly in *Return to Oz* (1985), styled after the original drawing by John R. Neill in *The Tin Woodman of Oz* (1918). [Left: © Walt Disney Productions. Right: courtesy of Contemporary Books Inc., Chicago.]

Murch first reread all the Baum Oz books and decided to make the second and third books into a single story. In January 1985, during a pause in dubbing his picture at London's Elstree Studios, he described why he and his co-writer, Gill Dennis, had done this.

"The second book (*The Land of Oz*) is a totally self-contained story which doesn't have anyone from the real world in it. Baum wrote the third book (*Ozma of Oz*) which has Dorothy's return to Oz, but the problem was that things had happened in Oz in her absence. Ozma had ascended to the throne in the second book. So Dorothy had to be brought up to date about what had happened while she was away. That seemed awkward to me, and I think if Baum had known he was going to write so many books he would have done it differently. What I've tried to do is to have Dorothy take an active part in the un-folding of the events of the second book so she's not a spectator; she's a central character."

Murch also made a team out of Tik-Tok and Jack Pumpkinhead, who came from different books. "They're very good foils for each other in the sense that one is the opposite of the other. Tik-Tok is solid, squat and heavy and is not alive, whereas Jack is tall, thin and flimsy and nothing but alive."

The script originally included parts of the eighth book, *Tik-Tok of Oz*, although now only some details amplifying Tik-Tok's character remain. On the other hand, Murch introduced many other Oz characters as briefly-glimpsed guests in his final Coronation sequence. He includes the one-legged Hip Hopper and the Patchwork Girl from *The Patchwork Girl of Oz*, and the multi-legged Johnny Kwikstep from *The Tin Woodman of Oz*.

Murch did not want to write a direct extension of the 1939 movie. He quickly decided against making his film a musical. He wanted to find "a different stylistic voice," but he had to take into account the deep regard for the earlier film. "You can't

deny it. It's part and parcel of people's mental baggage; it's part of the imaginative furniture of the twentieth century. So what I had to do was to harmonize with things that were part of the first film. I didn't want to play the same notes as the other film played. On the other hand, I didn't want to go off the keyboard and play something totally different."

That is why he retained the ruby color of Dorothy's slippers (this required negotiation with MGM, who initiated the change from silver). It also explains why Dorothy remains a brunette like Judy Garland's Dorothy rather than a blond as in the book. (This decision necessitated making Ozma blond rather than brunette for contrast.)

However, it was decided to cast a young girl as Dorothy, nearer to the age Baum had indicated in his books. Executive producer Gary Kurtz comments, "In the MGM film it didn't much matter because it was a theatrical vehicle — the vaudevillian approach to that was fine. To make her character work here, you really need the vulnerability of a child and her fears and anxieties."

Murch looked at a thousand applicants in seven or eight cities in the United States and Canada. Eventually the choice was Fairuza Balk, a 9-year-old from Vancouver who had appeared in one previous television program but was otherwise inexperienced. Walter Murch and others working on the film (like Justin Case, the Scarecrow) were impressed by how closely she came to identify with the characters. Her real concern for her fantastic friends is greatly beneficial to the movie.

The director insisted that the characters correspond in form as closely as possible to the John R. Neill drawings. "They made a huge impression on me when I read the books, in almost an equal proportion to the words. I didn't get around to reading *The Wizard of Oz* until much later, and I remember being disturbed by the way the Denslow characters looked. I didn't like the way the Tin Woodman looked, for example. He had a round skull-like back to his head whereas the Neill Tinman has a real tin can of a head, which I much prefer. If you loved the way the characters looked in the Neill drawings, you'll like — I hope — the way they look in the film."

Considerable research also went into the sets, particularly into the appearance of the Emerald City and the Royal Palace. It was decided to follow the overall style of

Dorothy, clutching Billina, enters the Royal Palace with Tik-Tok in *Return to Oz.*
[© Walt Disney Productions. Photographed by Barry Peake.]

the Chicago World's Fair of 1893 which had probably inspired Baum. It was a fantasy version of classical architecture — stately but light because of its festive adaptation.

Fidelity to John R. Neill's work imposed considerable demands on the special-effects team. Lyle R. Conway, as Creature Design Supervisor, was faced with the problem of Billina, the talking hen. He had worked on *The Muppet Show*, sculpting Miss Piggy for 2 years. And he had pioneered the development of animatronic characters for *The Dark Crystal*, using radio and cable control in new ways. So he was not unaccustomed to creative challenges.

A real hen was used in some shots, but Conway had to create a life-size replica that had over 100 moving parts in the head alone. The problem was more difficult than for an unreal creation because the hen had to move and act in a convincingly natural way.

For Tik-Tok, gymnast and dancer Michael Sundin was squeezed inside the

4½-feet tall figure to make him walk. All other actions were worked by remote control.

Will Vinton's clay animation techniques were applied to the Nomes so they could materialize out of walls. Ian Wingrove's expertise in mechanical effects was applied to the flight of the Gump, the makeshift flying contraption brought to life with a sprinkling of magic powder. Zoran Perisic solved the visual effects problems. These were associated with the flying sequences and with the cabinet room in which the film's Princess Mombi (based on Princess Langwidere in Baum's third book) takes off one head and tries on another from her collection.

Return to Oz was shot in England. Principal photography started on February 20, 1984. Britain was chosen to take advantage of the special effects expertise available there, not ignoring the favorable exchange rate with the dollar. Originally, other scenes were to be shot in Kansas, as well as Sardinia, Algeria, Spain and Rome.

Dorothy finds a lunchbox growing on a tree in *Return to Oz*. The scene follows the illustration by John R. Neill in *Ozma of Oz* (1907). [Left: © Walt Disney Productions.]

The Cabinet Room from *Return to Oz*. Here the evil Princess Mombi keeps her collection of heads which she can change at will. The character was originally Princess Langwidere in *Ozma of Oz*. The John R. Neill illustration shows her trying on her 19th head. [Film scene: © Walt Disney Productions. Photographed by Barry Peake.]

The budget climbed so high, however, that almost everything was done at the studio. (The army-training grounds on Salisbury Plain in southern England doubled for Kansas and were relatively close to the studio company's base at Elstree.) Even so, the total cost was $25 million.

The story of *Return to Oz* is a direct sequel to *The Wizard of Oz* book. It does not dismiss Oz as Dorothy's dream — Oz exists. Walter Murch remarks: "The problem at the beginning of the film is that Dorothy has been to Oz, yet she is living in Kansas. Everyone says to her, 'No, my darling, it was just a bump on the head. You had a bad dream. You imagined all this. It doesn't exist.' Yet it was such a powerful story for her, more powerful than reality, so she insists it was real. And that's the conflict the film begins with and the conflict that runs throughout the length of the film and is hopefully resolved in the end."

Return to Oz is, in the words of Gary Kurtz, "a realistic adventure fantasy." Dorothy's return to Oz is full of terror and

Dorothy with her Aunt Em (Piper Laurie) in *Return to Oz*.
[© Walt Disney Productions.]

excitement because she finds Oz has been conquered. "The problem at the end of the first film," says Walter Murch, "was that Oz was left in an unstable state. The Wizard left in a balloon, and the Strawman was on the throne. *Return to Oz* is about the dream destroyed. Her dream has been demolished, turned upside down. She not only has to restore her dream but also find a way to stabilize it, so when she goes back to Kansas it remains secure."

The new film was not designed as part of a series. Murch did not choose the second and third books in order to leave the next ones free for a sequel. He feels Baum had more difficulty writing the later Oz stories and says, "I would be hard put to extract a story of equal power from the later Baum books." Of course, if *Return to Oz* is a smash hit, sequels may be made, but Murch insists, "I would not be involved in any future Oz films. I've so enjoyed this that I wouldn't want to spoil it by going on with another one. This story definitely has to do with the *first* return. Can you go back after having had an experience like that? Is it recapturable? That's the theme that interests me, and how could I do that again? Would it be possible to recapture the recapturing of . . . .? No, it gets ridiculous after that."

Return to Oz had its full share of production problems. At one point, George Lucas and Francis Coppola flew over to support their friend Walter Murch when production had fallen behind schedule, and he had temporarily been fired. But many films are the better for such crises. After all, *The Wizard of Oz* had a complicated production history of its own.

Whatever else the film achieves, it has opened the eyes of the world to the dimensions of the Oz saga. And it has already alerted one independent producer to the further possibilities of Baum! He has commissioned a script from the non-Oz *The Sea Fairies* that could be filmed at the end of 1985. There is more to Oz than *The Wizard of Oz* — this is now common knowledge. Not since the appearance of MGM's 1939 movie has there been such a renewal of interest in the fantastic world created so many years ago by L. Frank Baum.

L. Frank Baum, creator of Oz, in a 1908 portrait. "Never question the truth of what you fail to understand," he once wrote, "for the world is filled with wonders."

APPENDICES

□□□□□□□□□□□ □□

Oz Books

A record of the principal works of fiction presenting the Land of Oz and its characters, listed in order of appearance. Many, of course, have appeared in numerous later editions and some in foreign languages.

By L. Frank Baum, illustrated by W.W. Denslow; published originally by George M. Hill Co.:

1900 **THE WONDERFUL WIZARD OF OZ**, later titled **THE NEW WIZARD OF OZ** and **THE WIZARD OF OZ.**

By L. Frank Baum, illustrated by John R. Neill; published originally by Reilly & Britton/Reilly & Lee:

1904 **THE MARVELOUS LAND OF OZ**, later known as **THE LAND OF OZ**
1907 **OZMA OF OZ**
1908 **DOROTHY AND THE WIZARD IN OZ**
1909 **THE ROAD TO OZ**
1910 **THE EMERALD CITY OF OZ**
1913 **THE PATCHWORK GIRL OF OZ**
1914 **TIK-TOK OF OZ**
1915 **THE SCARECROW OF OZ**
1916 **RINKITINK IN OZ**
1917 **THE LOST PRINCESS OF OZ**
1918 **THE TIN WOODMAN OF OZ**
1919 **THE MAGIC OF OZ**
1920 **GLINDA OF OZ**

By Ruth Plumly Thompson, illustrated by John R. Neill; published originally by Reilly & Lee:

1921 **THE ROYAL BOOK OF OZ** [credited to L. Frank Baum]
1922 **KABUMPO IN OZ**
1923 **THE COWARDLY LION OF OZ**
1924 **GRAMPA IN OZ**
1925 **THE LOST KING OF OZ**
1926 **THE HUNGRY TIGER OF OZ**
1927 **THE GNOME KING OF OZ**
1928 **THE GIANT HORSE OF OZ**
1929 **JACK PUMPKINHEAD OF OZ**
1930 **THE YELLOW KNIGHT OF OZ**
1931 **PIRATES IN OZ**
1932 **THE PURPLE PRINCE OF OZ**
1933 **OJO IN OZ**
1934 **SPEEDY IN OZ**

By Frank [Joslyn] Baum, illustrated by Milt Youngren; published by Whitman Publishing Co.:

1935 **THE LAUGHING DRAGON OF OZ**

By Ruth Plumly Thompson, illustrated by John R. Neill; published originally by Reilly & Lee:

1935 **THE WISHING HORSE OF OZ**
1936 **CAPTAIN SALT IN OZ**
1937 **HANDY MANDY IN OZ**
1938 **THE SILVER PRINCESS IN OZ**
1939 **OZOPLANING WITH THE WIZARD OF OZ**

By John R. Neill with his own illustrations; published originally by Reilly & Lee:

1940 **THE WONDER CITY OF OZ**
1941 **THE SCALAWAGONS OF OZ**
1942 **LUCKY BUCKY IN OZ**

By Jack Snow, illustrated by Frank Kramer; published originally by Reilly & Lee:

1946 **THE MAGIC MIMICS IN OZ**
1949 **THE SHAGGY MAN OF OZ**

By Rachel R. Cosgrove, illustrated by "Dirk" [Dirk Gringhuis]; published originally by Reilly & Lee:

1951 **THE HIDDEN VALLEY OF OZ**

By Eloise Jarvis McGraw and Lauren McGraw Wagner, illustrated by Dick Martin; published originally by Reilly & Lee:

1963 **MERRY GO ROUND IN OZ**

By Ruth Plumly Thompson, illustrated by Dick Martin; published by the International Wizard of Oz Club:

1972 **YANKEE IN OZ**
1976 **THE ENCHANTED ISLAND OF OZ**

By Eloise Jarvis McGraw and Lauren Lynn McGraw, illustrated by Dick Martin; published by the International Wizard of Oz Club:

1980 **THE FORBIDDEN FOUNTAIN OF OZ**

Oz Movies

□□

The following list includes the principal Oz productions for cinema and television. Details of some minor Oz films, and of announced films that were never made, can be found in "Oz on Film" compiled by Marc Lewis for the Winter, 1983 edition of *The Baum Bugle*.

1910
THE WIZARD OF OZ
Director/Screenwriter: Otis Turner.
Production Company: Selig. 1,000 feet of film.
Cast: Bebe Daniels (Dorothy), Hobart Bosworth, Eugenie Besserer, Robert Leonard, Winnifred Greenwood, Lillian Leighton, Olive Cox.

DOROTHY AND SCARECROW IN OZ
Production Company: Selig. 1,000 feet.

THE LAND OF OZ
Production Company: Selig. 1,000 feet.

1914
THE PATCHWORK GIRL OF OZ
Director: J. Farrell MacDonald.
Screenwriter: L. Frank Baum. Music (for live accompaniment): Louis F. Gottschalk. Production Company: Oz Film Manufacturing Co. Distributor: Paramount. 5 reels.
Cast: Violet MacMillan (Ojo), Frank Moore (Unc Nunkie), Raymond Russell (Dr. Pipt), Leontine Dranet (Margolotte), The Marvelous Couderc [Pierre Couderc] (Patchwork Girl), Bobbie Gould (Jesseva), Marie Wayne (Jinjur), Dick Rosson (Danx), Frank Bristol (Soldier with the Green Whiskers), Ben Deeley (Rozyn), Fred Woodward (Woozy/Zoop/Mule), Todd Wright (Wizard of Oz), Herbert Glennon (Scarecrow), Al Roach (Cowardly Lion), Andy Anderson (Hungry Tiger), Jessie May Walsh (Ozma), William Cook (Royal Chamberlain), Lon Musgrave (Tin Woodman).

HIS MAJESTY, THE SCARECROW OF OZ (later called THE NEW WIZARD OF OZ)
Director/Screenwriter: L. Frank Baum. Music (for live accompaniment): Louis F. Gottschalk. Production Company: Oz Film Manufacturing Co. Distributor: Alliance. 5 reels.
Cast: Violet MacMillan (Dorothy), Todd Wright (Pon), Vivian Reed (Gloria), Mai Wells (Mombi), Raymond Russell (King Krewl), Arthur Smollet (Googly-Goo), Mildred Harris (Button-Bright), Fred Woodward (Mule/Kangaroo/Cowardly Lion/Crow), Frank Moore (Scarecrow), Pierre Couderc (Tin Woodman), C. Charles Haydon (Wizard).

1925
THE WIZARD OF OZ
Director: Larry Semon.
Screenwriters: Larry Semon, L. Frank Baum Jr., Leon Lee. Distributor: Chadwick Pictures. 6,300 feet.
Cast: Larry Semon (Scarecrow), Bryant Washburn (Prince Kynd), Dorothy Dwan (Dorothy), Virginia Pearson (Countess Vishuss), Charles Murray (Wizard), Oliver N. Hardy (Tin Woodman), Josef Swickard (Prime Minister Kruel), Mary Carr (Aunt Em), G. Howe Black (Rastus), Frank Alexander (Uncle Henry), Otto Lederer (Ambassador Wikked), Frederick Ko Vert (Phantom of Basket). [As previously explained, Larry Semon and Oliver Hardy play farmhands who simply masquerade as a scarecrow and tin man for a short while.]

1939
THE WIZARD OF OZ
Director: Victor Fleming. Screenwriters: Noel Langley, Florence Ryerson, Edgar Allan Woolf. Music: Harold Arlen. Lyrics: E.Y. Harburg. Producer: Mervyn Le Roy. Production Company/Distributor: Metro-Goldwyn-Mayer. Technicolor. 100 minutes.
Cast: Judy Garland (Dorothy), Frank Morgan (Professor Marvel/Wizard), Ray Bolger (Hunk/Scarecrow), Bert Lahr (Zeke/Cowardly Lion), Jack Haley (Hickory/Tin Woodman), Billie Burke (Glinda), Margaret Hamilton (Miss Elvira Gulch/Wicked Witch), Charley Grapewin (Uncle Henry), Clara Blandick (Auntie Em), Pat Walshe (leader of Winged Monkeys), Toto (Toto).

1960
THE SHIRLEY TEMPLE SHOW — THE LAND OF OZ (television)
Director: William Corrigan. Writer: Frank Gabrielson. Producer: William Asher. Color (tape). 60 minutes (with breaks).
Cast: Shirley Temple (Tip/Ozma), Jonathan Winters (Nikidik), Ben Blue (Scarecrow), Sterling Holloway (Jack Pumpkinhead), Gil Lamb (Tin Woodman), Agnes Moorehead (Mombi), Frances Bergen (Glinda), Arthur Treacher (Nikidik's butler), Mel Blanc, Charles Boaz, William Keene.

1963
RETURN TO OZ (television)
Animation. Directors: F.R. Crawley, Thomas Glynn, Larry Roemer.
Writer: Romeo Muller. [This was an original sequel to *The Wizard of Oz* book.] Animators:

Barrie Nelson, Rod Willis, William Mason, Blake James, Don Stearn, Vic Atkinson, Milton Stein, George Rufle, George Germanetti, Angelo Terricone. Backgrounds: Dennis Pike and others. Music and lyrics: Gene Forrell, Edward Thomas, James Polack. Producers: Arthur Rankin Jr., Jules Bass. Color. 60 minutes (with breaks).
Voices: Susan Conway (Dorothy), Larry Hann, Alfie Scopp, Carl Banis, Susan Morse, Pegi Loder.

1969
THE WONDERFUL LAND OF OZ
[Based on the book *The Land of Oz*]
Director/Screenwriter/Producer: Barry Mahon. Songs: Loonis McGlohon, Alec Wilder. Production Company: Cinetron. Distributor: Childhood Productions. Color. 72 minutes.
Cast: Channy Mahon (Tip/Ozma), Joy Webb.

1971
JOURNEY BACK TO OZ
Animation. Director: Hal Sutherland. Writers: Fred Ladd, Norman Prescott, (additional dialogue) Bernard Evslin. Chief Animator: Amby Paliwoda. Songs: Sammy Cahn, Jimmy Van Heusen. Producers: Norman Prescott, Lou Scheimer. Production Company/ Distributor: Filmation Associates. Eastman Color. 88 minutes.
Voices (listed alphabetically): Milton Berle (Cowardly Lion), Herschel Bernardi (Woodenhead the Horse), Paul Ford (Uncle Henry), Margaret Hamilton (Aunt Em), Jack E. Leonard (Signpost), Paul Lynde (Pumpkinhead), Ethel Merman (Mombi), Liza Minnelli (Dorothy), Mickey Rooney (Scarecrow), Risë Stevens (Glinda), Danny Thomas (Tinman), Mel Blanc (Crow).
1971 is copyright date — released November 1974.

1976
OZ (Australian — shown in America as
20TH CENTURY OZ)
[suggested by *The Wizard of Oz*]
Director/Screenwriter: Chris Lofven. Music: Ross Wilson. Songs: Ross Wilson, Baden Hutchins, Gary Young, Wayne Burt. Producers: Chris Lofven, Lyne Helms. Production Company: Count Features. Distributor (U.S.A., 1977): Inter Planetary. Eastman Color. 102/103 minutes (U.S.: 85 minutes).
Cast: Joy Dunstan (Dorothy), Graham Matters (Wally/Wizard/record salesman/tram

conductor/doorman/face at party), Bruce Spence (bass player/surfie [equivalent to] Scarecrow), Michael Carman (drummer/ mechanic [equivalent to] Tin Woodman), Gary Waddell (guitarist/bikie [equivalent to] Cowardly Lion), Robin Ramsey (Good Fairy), Ned Kelly (truckie/bouncer), Lorraine West (waitress), Boris Underhill (hotel receptionist), Russell Thompson (1st gay), Gino Lattore (2nd gay), Paula Maxwell (Jane), Jim Slade (promoter), Roland Bonnet (manager), Stephen Millichamp, James Williamson and Phil Motherwell (truckies).

1978
THE WIZ
Director: Sidney Lumet. Screenwriter: Joel Schumacher (from stage production with book by William F. Brown and music and lyrics by Charlie Smalls; adapted from the book *The Wizard of Oz*). Songs: Charlie Smalls. Music Adaptation: Quincy Jones. Producer: Rob Cohen. Executive producer: Ken Harper. Production Company: Motown. Distributor: Universal. Technicolor. 134 minutes.
Cast: Diana Ross (Dorothy), Michael Jackson (Scarecrow), Nipsey Russell (Tin Man), Ted Ross (Cowardly Lion), Mabel King (Evillene [equivalent to] Wicked Witch of the West), Theresa Merritt (Aunt Em), Thelma Carpenter (Miss One), Lena Horne (Glinda the Good Witch), Richard Pryor (The Wiz), Stanley Greene (Uncle Henry), Clyde J. Barrett (Subway peddler).

1985
RETURN TO OZ
Director: Walter Murch. Screenwriters: Walter Murch, Gill Dennis (from the books *The Land of Oz* and *Ozma of Oz*, with details from *Tik-Tok of Oz*). Producer: Paul Maslansky. Executive producer: Gary Kurtz. Production Company: Oz Productions/Walt Disney Productions. Distributor: Buena Vista. Color. 120 minutes (approx.).
Cast: Fairuza Balk (Dorothy), Nicol Williamson (Dr. Worley/Nome King), Jean Marsh (Nurse Wilson/Mombi), Piper Laurie (Aunt Em), Matt Clark (Uncle Henry), Emma Ridley (Ozma), Michael Sundin and Peter Elliot (Tik-Tok), Pons Maar (leader of the Wheelers), Justin Case (Scarecrow), John Alexander (Cowardly Lion), Deep Roy (Tin Man), Sophie Ward (Mombi 1), Fiona Victory (Mombi 2). Jack Pumpkinhead performed by Brian Henson. Billina performed by Mac Wilson. Nomes (Claymation) by Will Vinton.

Writings About Oz

This book has only space enough to skim the literary background of the Oz books and the issues they raise for scholars. Major sources of additional information and evaluation of the Oz books and films and their creators include:

1954 **WHO'S WHO IN OZ.** By Jack Snow. (Reilly & Lee, Chicago.) Informal introductions to more than 630 Oz people, animals and creatures. Story-highlights of the 39 Oz books published from 1900 to 1951. Includes biographical sketches of their authors and illustrators.

1957 to date **THE BAUM BUGLE.** "A Journal of Oz," published regularly by the International Wizard of Oz Club. Covers all aspects of Oz, including the Club's activities. Eighty issues published by Autumn 1984 number, when subscriptions (including Club membership) were $10 each. Write: Fred M. Meyer, 220 North 11th Street, Escanaba, MI 49829.

1957 **THE WIZARD OF OZ AND WHO HE WAS.** By Martin Gardner and Russel B. Nye. (Michigan State University Press, East Lansing.)

1961 **TO PLEASE A CHILD.** By Frank Joslyn Baum and Russell P. MacFall. (Reilly & Lee, Chicago.) A biography of L. Frank Baum, co-written by Baum's eldest son.

1973 **THE ANNOTATED WIZARD OF OZ.** (Clarkson N. Potter, New York.) Contains a facsimile of the rare first edition with all the original drawings by W.W. Denslow in correct colors. Annotations to text by Michael Patrick Hearn, plus many additional illustrations. Includes an introduction to Baum and his book and an extensive bibliography (both by Hearn).

1974 **WONDERFUL WIZARD, MARVELOUS LAND.** By Raylyn Moore. (Bowling Green University Popular Press, Bowling Green, Ohio.)

1976 **W.W. DENSLOW.** By Douglas G. Greene and Michael Patrick Hearn. (Clarke Historical Library, Central Michigan University, Mt. Pleasant, Michigan.)

1976 **BIBLIOGRAPHIA OZIANA.** By Peter E. Hanff and Douglas G. Greene extending work by Dick Martin, James E. Haff and David L. Greene. (The International Wizard of Oz Club, Kinderhook, Illinois.) A concise bibliographical checklist of the Oz books by Baum and successors.

1976 **DOWN THE YELLOW BRICK ROAD: THE MAKING OF THE WIZARD OF OZ.** By Doug McClelland. (Pyramid Books, New York.) Details production of the 1939 film.

1977 **THE MAKING OF THE WIZARD OF OZ.** By Aljean Harmetz. (Alfred A. Knopf, New York.) Details production of the 1939 film.

1977 **THE OZ SCRAPBOOK.** By David L. Greene and Dick Martin. (Random House, New York.) Story of Baum and "Later Explorers of Oz." The iconography of Oz. Oz on stage and screen. Ozian artifacts. The Oz canon (listing of books). Profusely illustrated.

1978 **THE WIZ SCRAPBOOK.** By Richard J. Anobile. (A Berkley Windhover Book, New York.) Details production of the 1978 film.

1983 **THE WIZARD OF OZ.** By L. Frank Baum, with pictures by W.W. Denslow. Michael Patrick Hearn, Editor. (Schocken Books, New York.) Part of *The Critical Heritage* series. Original book and illustrations (not in color) with lengthy introduction by Hearn and long appendix of historical essays on Baum and the books, articles on librarians and Oz, and a selection of current criticism.